Advance Praise
Insider Secrets to Hit Songwrit

"Molly has written an excellent primer on the world of song-writing. It's a great resource for folks trying to navigate the 'how tos' of the songwriting business."

—Tim Wipperman, President, Anthem Music Publishing

"This is a wonderful book that offers superb advice to song-writers, new and experienced. Molly Leikin gives you solid, prac-tical information, whether you are writing and composing for yourself or the whole world. Listen to her advice. This book may well be your ticket to songwriting success!"

—Philip Lee Williams, award-winning novelist and poet

INSIDER
SECRETS
TO HIT
SONGWRITING
IN THE
DIGITAL AGE

INSIDER SECRETS TO HIT SONGWRITING IN THE DIGITAL AGE

MOLLY LEIKIN

PERMUTED
PRESS

A PERMUTED PRESS BOOK
ISBN: 978-1-63758-218-3
ISBN (eBook): 978-1-63758-219-0

Insider Secrets to Hit Songwriting in the Digital Age
© 2022 by Molly Leikin
All Rights Reserved

Cover Art by Tiffani Shea
Interior Design by Yoni Limor

PERMUTED
PRESS

Permuted Press, LLC
New York • Nashville
permutedpress.com

Published in the United States of America
1 2 3 4 5 6 7 8 9 10

For Jaci Paradis Lamont
My childhood BFF.
See if God will give you a few days off
And float you down to Santa Barbara.
I'm here, with our bikes,
And we can ride anywhere together.
Remember?

And for Barry Fasman,
The Foz
My precious arranger, inspiration, and friend.

TABLE OF CONTENTS

ACKNOWLEDGMENTS

While I was clawing my way through hopeless steel for representation, even with my pushy pen and distinguished resume, I was still sitting on a red curb, with my ideas for this manuscript in a brown FedEx box, waiting for the bus that never came.

But one sunny rainy day, a witty Facebook stranger introduced me to her agent, who wanted to represent my work.

That Facebook person is now my dear friend, Marlene Wagman-Geller, and our agent is Roger S. Williams.

Thank you, both. You're my guys. Blessings.

There wouldn't be a book without:

Jamie Lovett, Debbie Dubb, John Beal, Robin Urdang, Nils Larson, Ginny Milhoan, David Thordarson, Judith Claire, David Birken, Lerman & Sons, Todd Brabec, Jeff Brabec, Michael Silversher, Patty Silversher, Carl Sturken, Evan Rogers, Jim Andron, Art Munson, Tim Wipperman, J.P. Saxe, Debbie Hupp, Baby Bear, Neil Finestone, Michael Anderson, Jacob Hoye, Heather King, Tiffani Rudder, Allie Woodlee, Brandon Rospond, Jerry Corbetta, David Diamond, Booba Harowitz, Lani Levine spelled correctly, Mack David, Charlie Black, my Sycamore tree and Facebook friends.

> "Never believe anyone who tells you that you don't deserve what you want."

> —TAYLOR SWIFT

PREFACE

Songwriting isn't something you do. It's who you are.

Growing up in a frozen Canadian household where all media was for news only, when I played and sang my precious songs with my baritone ukulele, I was yelled at and pounded with silence.

"Shut up that goddamn banjo," was what I heard after writing a beautiful new tune. Those shrieks always made me cry. "Don't be so sensitive," was their 24/7 rant. I wished someone would say "Good for you," or "That one's so pretty," but no. "Shut up that goddamn banjo" stormed my ears.

It was no better in college. People actually moved out of Whitney Hall, our dorm, when I couldn't stop playing and singing. But once I moved to California, where writing songs was celebrated, I realized that the best part of me is my sensitivity, and without it, I'm just another pretty, witty face with a great leggings collection.

I have worked as an artist and with artists of one kind or another all of my adult life, and I feel confident in saying that a creative person who isn't creating can become physically and mentally ill.

I believe a writer needs to write. A painter needs to paint. A businessperson needs to biz. This is a fact—non-negotiable. It's the truth. Living a stale life is dying.

I use my world of ideas as a cozy, safe place I visit every day to make my life fuller and richer. As a consultant, it pleases me to help other people do the very same thing. I believe that a person who should be creating, who wants to be creating and isn't, is a time bomb waiting to explode. I've watched my own highs and lows, and now I can quickly diagnose the reasons for anger and tears. Am I writing or not? If not, I gently push myself into going to work and getting back up through the bad mood bottom.

In addition to the "danger" factor of a creative life lived as a "civilian," who squashes ideas, consider how many gifts we, as the general public, are being denied because someone in Cincinnati should be dancing to Swan Lake but is a computer nerd instead, working a real job with dental benefits.

We all need dentists. Especially those of us who underwrite cute Dr. Ward's summers in Sicily. But being creative means taking risks. Somewhere between the insecurity of "I'd really like to invent this thing" and seeing it successfully launched in the marketplace, there is a moment when you hold your breath and jump into your imagination, trusting it to guide your life.

I've always trusted my imagination to feed, house, clothe, chocolate, and entertain me; get me to yoga on time; and find me the right agent, publisher, recording artist to sing and perform my songs, and, especially, the right clients to truly benefit from my input.

My imagination has never let me down. I feel I have control over my creativity instead of being a victim to it. In this book, I show you how to do that too. And as a consultant, I've helped many thousands of other creative people—some of whom thought they might be tunesmiths but weren't sure—find their fingerprint as artists, and flourish.

Twelve of them are Grammy winners. Nineteen more are Grammy nominees. And so far, with my help, more than 7,500 other lyricists, singer/songwriters, and artists have placed their work in movies, TV shows, video games, and commercials, and their tracks are downloaded all over the web.

Are you next?

I wrote this book just for you.

INTRODUCTION

Songwriting is the most glorious and terrible thing I know. When gobsmacked by a great idea, I'm happy to let it keep me awake for as many nights in a row as my song needs, to grow into a contagious tune I absolutely can't stop singing. The thunder pumping through my veins stimulates me to stretch my shadow as I perfect and pamper my latest composition like a beloved, newborn baby.

Then there are those vicious, smarmy days when I'm stuck, when all I hear, if I even hear anything at all, are noes, nahs, get outs, and go to medical school. At that point, I'm one Snickers bar away from pureeing my keyboard, taking a rolling pin to my guitar, and setting fire to my idea book.

As devastating as that feels, somehow I always forget the negative side of songwriting as soon as the next idea floats into my honey vanilla chamomile tea. The thunder starts pumping again, I scramble for my pen, and I'm home.

Writing makes me, me. I feel whole and substantial in a way nothing else does. When I hear my music and lyrics on the air and online, or see my songs listed on the *Billboard* charts, I'm triumphant.

As for the tunes, tracks, and lyrics that nobody but me has ever heard, I cherish them too, and maybe love them a little more. The awards on my walls remind me that I've made the right choices, after all, at the crossroads of my life. There, I walked right by the signs pointing to safe, predictable sidewalks leading to paid holidays and pensions, and headed, instead, into the uncharted forests, singing.

Join me there, as you read this book.

> "You can't knock on opportunity's door
> and not be ready."
>
> —BRUNO MARS

From the day I wrote my first song, people have asked me if I came from a musical family. Here's what I tell them:

When my paternal grandfather, Louis Leikin, was born in Russia, his mother never registered his birth because she didn't want him to be conscripted into the army. Well, the day he turned fifteen, the Cossacks caught up with him and hauled him in for a physical.

Grampa was strong and healthy but managed to find the right guy to convince he was a violinist of exceptional ability. So he was told to come back the next day for an audition.

But alas, on audition day, Grampa Louis appeared with his hand in a cast. Although he couldn't play for the general, he was so convincing, he was assigned to the army band anyway.

A few days later, while the Russian musicians toured close to the Polish border, Grampa unzipped his cast, tossed away the violin he never knew how to play, jumped the fence, and ran until he found steerage passage to Canada.

So if you ask me if I'm from a musical family, I have to say, "Not really." I'm a songwriter because I wanted to be one. I was driven. I wouldn't accept anything less. I had to do this or die.

If you have that same fire burning in you, read on, and I'll show you how I did it, how the pros do it, and how you can do it too.

I created the industry of Song Consulting. Now there's someone on every corner trying to be me. As your personal, private Songwriting Consultant, I will guide you as you create market-ready lyrics, melodies, and tracks, then help you get them to all the right people.

Are you next?

My money's on you.

CHAPTER 1

HOW TO WRITE A HIT LYRIC

SONG STRUCTURE

Some of you write lyrics. Others write melodies and tracks. Some write words, music, sing, and produce. Whatever you contribute is essential.

To become a successful songwriter, it's important to know how to structure the whole song, not only your portion of it. So if you write melodies/tracks, don't skip over the chapter on lyrics. And lyricists, pay close attention to the chapter on melody. You may think you don't need to know what your writing partner is doing, but you do. Someday, your co-writer may be stuck and really need your help.

Be prepared.

Okay? Let's go.

HOW TO WRITE LYRICS

A lyric consists of the words the singer sings. It expresses what you feel. Intensely.

A good lyric tells a good story. A good story tells us something new, something only you can tell us because nobody but you, is you.

By definition, a story has a beginning, middle, and end. It answers the five Ws, plus how: who, where, what, when, why, and how. If you answer all of those questions in your story, it will be stronger than if you only answer a couple.

Here's one story:

A boy had a dog, the dog ran away. The boy had a dog, the dog ran away. The boy had a dog, the dog ran away.

We have the beginning of the story here, but that's all. Your audience wants to hear the rest of it.

Here's another story:

A boy had a dog, the dog ran away, the boy was terrified. He called the pound, the police, he hung signs on every tree and telephone pole in the neighborhood. He rode up and down, up and down every street in the neighborhood, calling the dog's name, day after day after day.

Finally, the boy flung himself on his bed, knowing he'd never see his pet again, and cried himself to sleep. When he woke up, the dog was licking his face.

THIS story answers all the Ws, plus how.

Without looking back, write down what you saw when you read the second story.

The more visual your writing, the easier it is to remember. Many of my clients call this the Telephone Pole Story, because that's what they remember seeing after they read all the way through.

When writing a song, your goal is to get your audience's attention and keep it to the end of the song. When sung, this story is something you can hear as well as see. The more senses it appeals to, the better. Therefore, when writing the stories to your songs before you create the lyrics, write as visually as possible. Your work will have double the impact.

Hundreds of lyricists come to me for consultation each month, sending word sheets with great beginnings that stop cold. That's a function of not having a strong story to tell. I created the exercise below to keep "stuck" out of your writing process.

FOUR EASY STEPS TO WRITING A HIT LYRIC

1. Put your title at the top of a blank page. Scribble down everything—absolutely everything—that comes to mind that you might want to include in a story with that title. There are no wrong answers. Don't cross anything out. Let it roll. Keep adding to the list and hang it on your fridge.

   Here's an example:

   Title: Pumpkin

   Met at Trader Joe's.
   Choosing a pumpkin.
   Orange, white, or green gourd?
   Round, huge, tiny, several?
   Bought 'em all.
   I invited you over.
   Made a fire.
   Carved on my back step.
   Hot cider—with a kick.
   Pumpkins smiled.
   Like us.
   Carved 'em together—with our initials too.
   Candles inside—glowing like us.
   Made love in their glow.
   Beautiful—like us.
   Then candles burned out.

Like us.
So sad.
Everyone else—festive.
Every September—pumpkins everywhere.
Wish you'd come back.
We'd go back to TJs.
To buy one more pumpkin.
And one more.
And one more.
Add candles—never go out.
You'd stay with me forever.
Even when it wasn't pumpkin time.

2. Put your title at the top of another blank piece of paper on your fridge. Go through your scribble list and circle the ideas you may want to include in your story, then write a few sentences in the form of a casual letter that doesn't rhyme, saying what's in your heart on that subject. This is not your doctoral thesis. Just say what you feel, following the example below. When that flow of ideas feels complete, move on to step three.

   I went to Trader Joe's to buy a pumpkin. You were there, too, doing the same thing. Neither of us could decide which one. I chose yours. You chose mine. You brought them over to my house so we could carve them together.

   You stayed. You lit a fire. We carved by its light. Drank hot cider with a kick. Put candles in our pumpkins. Made love in their glow.

   Next morning, you were gone.

3. Using another piece of blank paper, with the title on top, write a non-rhyming lyric about the title using the info from step three.

I needed a pumpkin
Went to Trader Joe's
You needed a pumpkin, too
I bought yours, you bought mine
At my place, we carved them, and made
love in their glow
I've never been so happy
CHORUS:
Orange, yellow, green, and white
Huge and tiny, striped and dots
Piled upon those bales of hay
I'll never forget
Then you up and disappeared
Now every fall at Trader Joe's
I wonder if the season
Reminds you of me
Or am I just another fuzzy memory (that's)
CHORUS:
Orange, yellow, green, and white
Glowing in their candlelight
Huge and tiny striped and then
Could we do it all again.

4. Put your title on yet another piece of paper and write your rhyming lyric, the real lyric.

Your assignment is to finish the final draft of "Pumpkin."

When I create a lyric, I always write the story first so I know where I'm going.

Most of my lyricist clients who get stuck in verse one and don't know what else to write about as the song progresses don't have enough story. I send them back to who, where, what, when, why, plus how. THEN their story flows and so does their lyric.

A contemporary hit song is usually two and a half to three minutes long. Every song, whether written by Drake, Finneas/Billie Eilish, or Keith Urban, has a specific structure: a musical, lyric, and rhythmic pattern that repeats, usually twice, until time is up.

A hit song needs focus. We have to know immediately what it's about. Set up your story in the first line. Each line after that should be related to the title, adding something to embellish and enhance our understanding of the subject. Aim for something we haven't heard before.

LOVE SONGS

Most hit songs are love songs. I love you, I hate you. I wish I could hate you. Stay away. Come back on Thursdays. I filed a restraining order. I rescinded it, so meet me at midnight. I made your favorite ribs, but sprinkled in a touch of cyanide. Some version of these. Just remember that your job as an artist is to tell us something new, not recycle what you've already heard.

As you're writing, ask yourself these five tough questions:

1. Have I heard this before?

2. If so, could I make it a little different?

3. If not, could I write something else?

4. Would I say this if I were talking to a friend on the phone?

5. If not, how would I say it?

These questions will keep you from recycling what other artists have already written. You have a fingerprint as a person and as a tunesmith. Write your fingerprint.

WHAT'S YOUR SONG ABOUT?

If you were writing a song about shoes, you'd probably include some mention of stilettos, soles, soles with holes, leather, patent leather, different brands like fancy Christian Louboutin, then Payless, New Balance, Coach, Cardin, boots, booties, sneakers, scruffs, worn-down heels, sizes, corns, bunions, and sandals. You wouldn't toss in a line about Amtrack unless you lost one of your shoes on a train.

When deciding what to write, choose a theme and stick to it. It's like watching a short movie. Say you're focusing on a boxer who gets a shot at the title. Nearly every scene and line of dialogue in that story would deal with the man's quest for victory. It wouldn't wander off on a tangent of things to do with string. The focus would stay on the boxer's dream.

It is the same with the story of your lyric but with far fewer words.

PARTS OF A SONG

In any genre, there are three essential parts to contemporary chart songs.

- The rhythm
- The melody
- The lyric

Songwriters need all three.

These days, rhythm is a thousand times more important than it used to be. Listen to "Fancy Like" by Walker Hayes on YouTube. Try not to sing along. I bet you're up, dancing, and singing the harmony by the middle of line one.

Let's break down song structure further.

There's a verse, a chorus, and a bridge.

Usually, the form is verse/chorus, verse/chorus, bridge/chorus.

The rhythm in the verse, the chorus, and the bridge are all different from one another.

The notes of the verse, the chorus, and the bridge are also all different from one another.

The words of the verse, the chorus, and the bridge are all different from one another too.

The chords of the verse, the chorus, and the bridge are different from those in the rest of the song.

Carve that in stone.

WHAT IS A LYRIC?

A lyric is what a singer sings. So do you, whether or not you're a vocalist.

Similar to a traditional poem in that it often rhymes and has rhythm, the likeness ends there. A contemporary set of words for a song is usually conversational, something you'd say while talking to a friend on the phone. Keats and Shelley would probably plotz. But Blake Shelton and Dua Lipa would high-five each other.

Different from a traditional poem, as in an old-school Hallmark card, or *The Rime of the Ancient Mariner*, the rhythm and number of lines in a contemporary lyric is **not** consistent all the way through.

It is not:

I ran along the hall

My yellow shoes are small

I tripped on Bugaloo

As you my friend did, too

It's more like this:

> Ah – I see y'down the hall, dude
> Slippin' out
> Every day I love you more and more and
more
> I couldn't do it less.

Adding extra syllables, and taking some out, plus adding an extra line, makes your song more interesting. When your audience expects it to go left, steer your song right. As an artist, your job is to surprise us. If we know what's coming, we'll get bored and disappear. So keep it surprising.

In a lyric, the verse section has rhythm A. The chorus, rhythm B. The bridge, rhythm C. Be sure to use all three of your ABCs.

COLORS AND SHAPES

To simplify this, I assign each section a color. The verse is red, the chorus blue, the bridge green.

Let's go one step further and assign each colored section a shape. The verse is a red triangle, the chorus is a blue square, and the bridge a green circle.

Now that you know your lyrics need those three different rhythms, colors, and shapes, build them into your songs.

INSPIRATION

As a writer, I'm always happily stunned by good writing, no matter which form it takes. Whether it's Katie Couric's memoir, or Amanda Gorman's poetry, Luke Combs's song "One Margarita," penned by Michael Carter, Josh Thompson, and Matt Dragstrem, or Tim McGraw's "God Moves the Pen," written by James Slater and Tony Lane, or Walker Hayes's "Fancy Like."

Words are powerful. Since I'm an assignment writer, I know in advance where my song is going. I suggest choosing a target for your songs, too, before you start to write. Imagine you've been commissioned to write a song for a brand-new restaurant chain that's about to launch.

Say your song is about a restaurant. Do this exercise.

THE RESTAURANT EXERCISE

On a clean sheet of paper, or on your phone or iPad/computer, write the words "My Restaurant" at the top. Then list every picture or feeling those words evoke in you. Ask a lot of questions, like the ones below, and answer them using your imagination.

> What is the name of this restaurant? Tell me something new.

> In what location? On this planet? If not, where?

> What color(s) is the door?

> What color are the chairs? Are there chairs? If not, what?

> What color/texture is the floor? Is there one?

> Is it wood? Cement, carpeted? Do you wade in water to get to your table? Do you have to row your own kayak to get there?

> What color are the forks?

Spoons?

What kind of imaginary food is served there? Don't tell me hamburgers or hot dogs. This is your made-up meal. Make it fun.

What makes this restaurant unusual? Does it float above the telephone wires?

When you walk by on the sidewalk, what do you smell?

Is there a maître d' or a squawk box, like at McDonald's?

Is it a walk-in, walk-up, drive-through?

Are there bananas hanging from the ceiling? If so, what colors, and which flavors? Don't tell me what I'm expecting to hear.

What are the servers' uniforms? Not black and white. Tell me something new. Use your imagination.

All the servers have three left hands. What else is unusual about them?

What languages do they speak? French, Spanish, Thai, or K'moosh moosh? Say "I'm hungry" in each language.

Is the menu on the wall? Is it written on a chalk board too? In crayon on a linen tablecloth?

What's the unusual house specialty during your visit? Use your imagination.

Do they use plates, or do they tie your hands behind your back and you eat your meal like a puppy?

Do you have to order off the menu, or can you imagine a concoction, snap your fingers, and poof—there's your dinner?

If they serve ice cream, what's the most unusual flavor? Peppermint/chili, kale/rubber tire, or make one up.

How do you pay for your meal? Not with a credit card, check, or ATM, cash, Venmo, PayPal, Zelle, Bitcoin or any existing apps. Make up something new.

If you don't finish your meal, what happens? Does it evaporate? Does it get droned and dropped next to a hungry child at a bus stop?

Since they don't take reservations, what do you do while waiting for a table? There are no cell phones, computers, tablets, or other tech gadgets for you to play with.

While waiting to be seated, do you plop yourself down in the garden and practice yoga, do pushups? Give yourself a pedicure? Using what?

Congratulations! You did it.
I'm proud of you for using your imagination.
Here's another visual exercise.

"THROUGH MY WINDOW I SEE." EXERCISE

Sometimes, I only see our Santa Barbara chamber of commerce blue sky. At other times, during the day, through my off-white, half-open wood blinds, I also see:
My blooming camelia bush with hot pink flowers.
The curving pebble path next to my precious succulent garden.
Wood chips where our immaculate golf green-like lawn used to be before the draught when the State of California demanded we dig up the grass.

My *Los Angeles Times*, strategically plopped by the delivery person in its daily puddle, waiting for me to come out to pick it up without getting mad.

A smooth, black-topped driveway bordered by a wide purple morning glory hedge, turning from pink to purple as the sun moves west.

Joggers, skateboarders, seniors in matching khakis holding hands with their spouses.

A curly little girl on her first pink bike with her daddy cheering her on.

A rattling, beat-up, black '76 Ford gardening truck trailing blue smoke.

I could've said I just saw trees and a driveway. When I added the details, see how much more interesting it got? Don't forget the details.

What do you see from your window? Details, please.

For the next few lyrics you write, pick someone in the top forty now and write your songs for that artist. Even if you sing your own songs, pretend, for one exercise, that you don't, and compose something for somebody else who is a mainstream verse/chorus artist. Make it sound like that artist, not you.

WRITE YOUR FINGERPRINT

Don't recycle the same old, same old words you hear in every ordinary song. Trounce the clichés. You have a fingerprint unlike anybody else's on the planet. Write that. Write you.

LANGUAGE

Nobody creating a new song now, in any genre, would ask, "Wither thou goeth, dude?" Instead, we ask, "Where y'headed?" That wither business pretty well packed up and left after the New Testament and some classic hymns.

As you can see from that example, it's important for you to develop an ear for how we talk now, one on one—not in stilted dialogue, or how people spoke decades or light-years ago. Now.

We wouldn't say, "Come hither, thy evening repast awaits." Now it's "Dinner's ready!"

In contemporary song lyrics, sing what you say.

REGIONAL DIALECTS

I love listening to the way people talk in different parts of the country and the world. Growing up in Canada, I saw cars parked in the *laneway*, not the driveway, as we call it in California. Here, we say, "Come over for dinner." In other parts of the country, it's supper. Our Brit cousins use torches in the dark, but in the USA, we refer to them as flashlights.

Language is fascinating. Just be sure you aren't addressing HRH Prince William with "Dude, bring beer, biatch, and hang out." (Actually, the heir to Britain's throne would probably love it.) In real life, you would probably address him this way: "Your Royal Highness, the pleasure of your company is requested for a knock-down, blow out, beer brawl at Nunzio's."

Your lyrics are dialog for singers. Make your words sound like something the singers would really say. If they don't, change them so they do. Easy.

Just as there are lots of cringe lyrics out there that embarrass me as a career craftsperson, there are some great sets of song words that make me proud to hold a hallelujah pencil. They include "One Margarita," "God Moves the Pen," "Fancy Like," and "drivers license."

PARODY ASSIGNMENT

After locating the lyrics to your favorite song at one of the thousands of sites online, I want you to do a search for the corresponding videos on YouTube and sing along. Hearing those words with those rhythms and melodies, you'll be inspired. And excited.

When you find the video or mp3 of your favorite current song, write a new lyric to it, putting one syllable of yours where one exists in the original song. Choose nonsense words so you aren't intimidated by the real ones (e.g., grapefruit skateboard in striped armadillos on purple Wednesdays). Play at it. Have fun. You'll surprise yourself. (Just remember, it's someone else's melody, which you can't keep. You're only using it as a model.)

Even now, I use this exercise when I'm assigned a great melody that needs words and I'm having trouble finding them. It always works for me. And it's an assignment I gave to my talented students at UCLA and still give it to my private clients all these years later.

When you complete it, you'll have a perfectly structured, new lyric. Now, you can write a REAL song to that same melody. But be aware, that tune is not available to you. But it's great practice.

CONTEMPORARY LANGUAGE

You'll see two sets of words below. One is a stilted condolence card, like you'd find at a traditional greeting card site or stand. The other is a contemporary lyric. Read and feel the difference.

TRADITIONAL GREETING CARD

Condolences I send to you
I know you're blue and miss your love so
true
But someday in the hereafter perhaps you
will see him
Even if it feels grim

However, if this were written in contempo-
rary form, it would read:
I send you my condolences
Knowing how deeply your loss goes
But I believe you'll meet again someday
Blessings.

Here's a more contemporary way of saying goodbye. It's the
chorus below:

I'll never say rest peacefully
'Cause how will you remember me?
If I delete your number
Your lifetime, always number
From my phone
I won't know who to be alone
Through my scowling, dirty windowpane
I'll look for you
And look for you
And next time through
Will you come home
To look for me?

© Molly-Ann Leikin

See the difference between a corny poem where the lines are turned around to force a rhyme, versus an emotional, stainless steel lonely lyric? Strive for the latter in your writing. Bleed on the paper.

COLLOQUIAL

The words to contemporary songs are colloquial and gush with emotion. Sometimes they rhyme, the lines are different lengths, but first, the feelings pour out, uncensored, exactly the way we feel them and speak about them.

Studying the marketplace, as I do daily, **that's** what you should be going for.

Your models are the top forty each week in your genre. Study them.

THE CHORUS

In any genre, the chorus is like a nursery rhyme for adults. Let's study "Ring Around the Rosie." It repeats, and the rhymes make it fun to recite and the far side of impossible to forget. Try writing a few silly syllable choruses like this. It'll be a nice change of pace from the "I gotta gotta write a hit."

> Ring around the Rosie
> A pocket full of posies
> Husha husha we all fall down.

This could be:

> Bought a bag of juju's
> Choc'late wiry dudu's
> Bambo, hambo we all paint socks.

It means absolutely nothing, but it's fun to write and sing.

Do this exercise even if you think it's dumb. It's meant to show you how much easier it is to write when the "should's" go away and you are "allowed" to be silly.

Try it.

WHAT AM I SUPPOSED TO SAY IN MY LYRIC?

Write what you feel.

Most hit songs are love songs, but if you want to write about your growling dishwasher, fine. Besides being vehicles for us to express ourselves, songs serve as a way to share our feelings with our audience. In order to make sure we *have* one, our job is to hook 'em. And once we do, we don't ever want to let them get away. Not even one person.

FORMAT

Beginning songwriters often fall into the trap of making their work too symmetrical. They feel if the first line of their song has eight beats, each of the following lines in that section has to match. It was almost mandatory at one time, but not anymore. Lyrics these days are much more interesting when the number of lines per section, along with the number of syllables per line, is different but match in corresponding verses.

So instead of four lines, four lines, four lines, change it up to five lines, 3.5 lines, six lines.

And to move it one step further:

Line one has seven syllables.

Line two, six.

Line three, six.

Line four, nine.

Line five, three.

What? Did she lose it altogether? Jeeze. That sure isn't very many syllables. How on earth am I going to say anything?

You're writing a song, not a novel. This exercise will show you the importance of each syllable you **don't** use. Imagine you're buying each syllable with $1,000 cash. No ATM. No credit cards, Venmo, Zelle, or any other digital app. Cash. This is a challenge for the talented writers whose lyrics are acres of words, two or three pages long. In that case, keep your long lines intact *for now*, and write a short, rhythmic chorus that is sing-songy, with repeating sounds, like nursery rhymes for adults.

Be playful. Less is more. Use syllables that don't make sense or tell a story in your just-for-fun draft. Here's mine:

> Gooey schmooey di doh spoon (7)
> I am almost lilac (6)
> You are typing toenails (6)
> We are wiggy jiggy smiggy lawns (9)
> Lucky us (3)

Alert the media!

I wouldn't bet on hearing that song at the Grammys anytime soon, or on The Weeknd's greatest hits, but it was fun to write. Throughout my creative day, I scribble down nonsense lines, even on the walls, to keep my mindset playful. I want you to do that too.

Now, write your silly lyric with seven, six, six, nine, and three syllables.

As you do, imagine you're giving yourself $1,000 cash for each syllable you **remove**. Sound more interesting now? Especially to those of you with the acres of words? Try it.

Here's my bulky acres of words lyric:

> Heaven help me, oh my God, my God my
> God we had a knock down drag out fight again
> I remember dancing in Miami on the dreamy
> South Beach sand all night way back then
> Now each evening light bulbs burst and

      pop and burst and burst above my bed
        When I can't stop no I can't drown the
      slimy hateful words you said

Another version is:

      We had another fight
      In Miami last night
      And nothing will squash your hateful words

Here's another short, singalongable chorus I wrote. See how few syllables it takes to say something:

      Turn the moon, the moon around
      So I can see it shine
      To lead my baby ho-oh-ome
      Remind him, remind him, he's he's—mine

CHORUS EXERCISE

Write a short, singalongable chorus after your long lines. While you do that, feel the rhythm, not just the rhymes.

WRITE OR FIND THE MELODY FIRST

If the tunes come first, my songs are always stronger melodically. If the words do, I tend to develop Iambic Pentameter Disease.

        EG: the <u>boy</u> on his <u>bike</u> rode a<u>head</u> of the
    <u>bus</u> down the <u>street</u>.

   Or

        <u>Wish</u> I could, <u>wish</u> I could, <u>wish</u> I could <u>be</u>
    someone <u>else</u>.

We speak English in iambic pentameter, so it's natural for us to write in it too. But it's deadly boring. No surprises. So even when my co-writers want some words to jumpstart our song, I have to force myself to vary the number of lines, and especially the lengths of them.

Here's a TERRIBLE lyric with four "aining" rhymes in a row.

> I miss you baby and it's raining
> Baby that's no-braining
> From love I am refraining
> My dreams you are a-staining

Yuck.

I suggest limiting your rhymes to two in a row. After the second line, change the sound. For example, after "ings" go to "oohs," to "aahs," then "ongs." And throw in an "o" where you least expect to hear one. Then ask yourself, how would I say this if I were speaking to a friend, or crying to an 800-prayer number?

This works better:

> Since you left skid marks on my heart
> Night and day feel the same
> They both feel like nothin'
> They're just different colors
> 'Cause you're blocked-my-number-gone
> Gone forever gone.

The lyric above sounds way more contemporary and could work in several genres, not just country. However, please note you can use it as a model, but can't keep it because it's mine.

NO LIFE, NO LOVE

Avoid using life as a rhyme word—please. If you use the obvious rhymes of wife, knife, strife, and fife, you'll lapse into clichés, and you're too good a writer for that. If you use "life," do so in the middle of a line:

> I love my life with you

It's easy to find an "ooh" rhyme that isn't predictable.

See what I mean?

And while you're at it, avoid using love as a rhyme word too. The limited, obvious rhymes are turtle dove, shove, glove, and of. Whoopie. They're predictable. You hear one, you know what's coming. But you're too good a writer for that, aren't you?

So put love in the middle of a line:

> I wish I didn't love you anymore.

Here's a goodbye lyric without the word love in it.

Temporary

> Now what?
> Who's next?
> I got your tacky tacky goodbye text.
> Stay gone
> Long gone
> Let some girl with bigger boobs
> Way big, big, bigger boobs
> Sign on
> But tell her goin' in
> —You're temporary

See how interesting the rhythm in "Temporary" feels? Did you expect it?

I had to fight my iambic pentameter devils. But I did it. So can you.

LISTEN TO THE COLORS

In the first songwriting class I attended, our teacher projected a well-known lyric on a big screen. He approached it with a box of magic markers, telling us if our lyrics sounded bland to add some color.

Ever since, I've been using this exercise for my own writing and giving it to my clients. With my permission, several of my colleagues are also using it.

Color each single rhyme (broke, cloak) in red, each double rhyme (hi there, bye bear) in green, each triple rhyme (banana, Savannah) in blue. Circle all the picture words (Tesla, sofa) in yellow. Color alliterations (cathedral, canoe) in turquoise. Then, for repeating lines, use purple. Finally, highlight inner rhymes (I met you **in** the fall, the **tin** roof sang **in** the rain) with pink.

The more colorful and illegible the lyric is, the better. If you just have a series of red underlines and your song doesn't sizzle yet, perhaps you need to add a color from a picture or a double rhyme. I like to shoot for at least three colors in each of my lyrics, and I suggest you do the same.

By the way, I always try to include a picture. That way, my words are appealing to two senses—sight and sound.

Which strikes you harder? Loving you is difficult, or "Love is Chocolate Chips & Quicksand"? (Steve Lawford and I already wrote that one.)

I bet you chose the latter.

FIVE SENSES EXERCISE

Write a song that includes all five senses. This one isn't for Record of the Year. It's just for you to try to stretch your shadow. Use sound, sight, touch, smell, and taste.

Example: the screaming polka dot coyote just barbecued pillowcases with prickly buns, singing The Lord's Prayer in chartreuse.

THE LYRIC PARODY EXERCISE

Write a new lyric to the melody of "God Moves the Pen," a big hit for Tim McGraw, written by James Thomas Slater and Tony Mac Lane. To me, *this* is a song! Make sure your lyric has nothing to do with the original.

You can find it on YouTube.

CLICHÉ CONTROL

For a songwriter convention in Hollywood, I created a product called Cliché Control. It was a small spray bottle with magic blue eau de tap in it. You sprayed some on your song. If clichés appeared, you rewrote your song. Then you sprayed it again. If clichés still appeared, you contacted me for a lyric consultation.

I wish I hadn't sold out because I need it now more than ever. There is a tendency among all writers to use clichés, phrases we've heard over and over again in songs, but which shouldn't be there. "I'm on the shelf," "I'm blue," and "morning light" are some that come immediately to mind. They cause the same negative response in me as fingernails scratching a blackboard. The true test of whether a word or phrase should be in a lyric is NOT whether you can get away with it because somebody famous did, but if you're saying something **new** and it sounds as natural as conversation.

Like most creative people, I've felt alone and expressed that isolation in a thousand ways. But I've never said, "I'm on the shelf." That is an expression that was acceptable in the forties and may still be lurking around, but ONLY because it rhymes with "self" and nothing else does.

Just because a word rhymes is not a good reason to use it. It has to say what you mean. I've never used the phrase. None of my successful colleagues have, either. Therefore, it doesn't belong in our songs. If you want to say that you've been by yourself and make it rhyme, trying some version of "I've been alone" instead. That sounds much more natural and leaves you many more choices for rhymes. Get off your shelves and write in the vernacular.

Like many artists, I'm moody, and whenever I've been unhappy, I've told my friends, "I'm depressed," "I'm bummed," "I'm way down." I've never said, "I'm blue." That, too, is a dated cliché. Nobody manufactures antidepressants for people suffering from that symptom.

We're writing songs for now, so our lyrics should sound contemporary. I've heard some wonderful, seductive lines in my life, but no man has ever asked me to stay with him 'til the "morning light." I have heard "I want to hold you all night" or "Please don't go home 'til tomorrow," but I've never heard this "morning light" phrase anywhere except in a tired lyric that didn't try hard enough to say something new.

One of Leikin's Laws is to sing it like you say it. If you wouldn't say it, don't sing it either.

Here's a song I love that I co-wrote, which is cliché-free. "Somewhere Left of Texas" is a solid verse/chorus, verse/chorus/bridge/chorus structure. You can hear it here, with the lyrics: https://songmd.com/song-player at songmd.com under Molly's Songs.

The title was buried in a lyric a client sent to me for consultation. I screamed when I saw it. My assistant thought something terrible happened and came running with a fire extinguisher. I showed her the words, and she was as excited as I was.

Before this lyric arrived in my inbox, I'd only heard of people driving north, east, south, or west of anywhere. But never "left." *That's* what got me. I also love the fact that "eh" in left was an internal rhyme with the "eh" in Texas.

After I asked my client if I could help him revise the words and write an original melody; we penned this:

"Somewhere Left of Texas"
Molly Leikin/Bob Algie

I was out of gas
The triple A was slow
It was raining, I was freezing
You pulled up and smiled, let's go
I'm not sure of anything else
Except I was with you
'Never been a person these things happen to
(happen to)
We went
CHORUS:
Maybe east, maybe north, maybe south
southwest
Hang a U, run a light, ripping 93
Up a hill, cross a bridge, shining in the sun
Somewhere left of (somewhere left of)
Texas.
All the stars came out
Every light was green
Our connection was a blessing
With pure hot lightning in between
Just when I was feeling sure that we'd go
on and on (and on)

I turned to say I love you
But you had up and gone (up and gone)
You went
CHORUS:
Maybe east, maybe north, maybe south
southwest
Hang a U, run a light, ripping 93
Up a hill, cross a bridge, shining in the sun
Somewhere left of (somewhere left of)
Texas
BRIDGE:
Maybe I dreamed the whole thing
Maybe I'll never know
But I'll always miss you
CHORUS:

© Red Amaryllis Music

Note: I live a good life. I make a comfortable living doing what I love to do. My home is beautiful and filled with light. My succulent garden continues to surprise me. I never have to go to the same old homogenized workplace and lose two hours of my life every morning on fuming freeways, then get trapped in the same brain-boggling morass eight hours later to go home and growl.

I'm healthy. Most of the time, I set my own work schedule. I meet wonderful creative people, they get deals, my friends laugh at my jokes, and everybody loves my sour cream cinnamon-raisin coffee cakes, nuts optional. My clients are nominated for, and win, Grammys. I write beautiful rhythmic songs that are placed in movies and TV shows. I'm in charge. And I'm free.

But the rest of the world is stuck. Responsibilities tie them down. Here at six. There at 6:18. Somewhere else at 6:22. Shop.

Cook. Dry cleaning. Oil change. Pick up at soccer. Remedial math homework. Banking error. Buy dinner fixings. Get Zoom working. Homework. Conference. Maybe watch a romantic comedy for four minutes until the water pipe breaks.

Stuck.

That's why Algie and I wrote "Somewhere Left of Texas."

It tells a new story. It's extremely visual, emotional, and does something we're not supposed to do but dream of doing anyway: running off on with a stranger and que sera, sera.

Without wasting a syllable, the story begins with "I was out of gas, the Triple A was slow." Then, it gets more desperate, with "it was raining, I was freezing," and then bam—when the singer was most vulnerable, "You pulled up and smiled, let's go."

No matter where the singer had come from, or what was going on in her life before she left home, at that moment, she was completely helpless. Then along comes a good Samaritan, and hey—did she have any other options?

She wasn't the kind of person who ran off with strangers, ever, but in that moment, when she was sure she'd perish out there alone in the freezing rain, she gave it up to the Universe and off she went with the guy with that nice smile.

Telling where they went (or was it where they might have gone?) she sings about going east, north, south, southwest, and LEFT of Texas, a direction she'd never been before. Have any of us? Was it New Mexico and the art of Santa Fe, Arizona and the Grand Canyon, California and the Redwoods? She didn't tell us for sure, but there are a lot of possibilities in our minds.

They went up a hill, crossed a bridge, racing at ninety-three miles per hour. And she had no idea where they were except it was *left* of Texas, bringing the story into a whole new dimension of fantasy, escapism, and romance.

Ah—romance—the magic word.

WRITE THE EXTREMES

On a scale of one to ten, with ten being the highest, most of us live our lives around a six. Nothing is terribly wrong and nothing is that good, either. It's a nice six. But when we play or watch sports, read books, go to the movies, and listen to music, on that scale of one to ten, audiences crave a plus or minus fifteen emotional extreme— the best thing that ever happened, or the worst.

If we write about the fives, so what? Nice. Pleasant, but so what? Our audience is hungry for us to take them on adventures that are plus or minus fifteens—or even higher.

That's what "Somewhere Left of Texas" is. For those among us who wouldn't dare run off with a stranger, I believe a good percent of you secretly love the possibility that maybe, just maybe, you might.

Between us, I had a secret email address, just in case Brad Pitt got bored with gorgeous and needed clever. But even though I kept moving up his waitlist, after Mark Cuban lost all that weight, I transferred my dreams to him.

We all have a secret somebody, right? Maybe MC was driving that car in "Somewhere Left of Texas." Who's driving in yours?

KEEP GOING

I'm well aware that some of you have been frustrated for a very long time, trying to make your good songs hit songs and get them to the right ears. But don't stop now.

As someone who went through everything you're going through, I don't want you to let your past attempts and near misses get in your way. The songs you wrote two or ten years ago that didn't make it have nothing to do with what you're doing now. As far as I'm concerned, they don't exist. We keep moving ahead, clean, without dragging disappointed baggage along. It isn't fair to contaminate your new work with the unfulfilled dreams and demands of your old material.

Be kind to yourself. Try to start fresh. Put away the fact that you've been writing for years and haven't gotten anywhere yet. By the time you finish this book, you'll have a lot of valuable information you never had before, or to which you weren't receptive. You'll be a better writer just for taking the initiative to find out what you could be doing that you're not doing. That's a tremendous step.

If you reward yourself sufficiently, your creative ego will be happy to step up the next time you set out to write your feelings down. It will be a little easier because you've already done it and acknowledged it with something immediate and tangible. Be sure to reward yourself for everything—every little thing you write—a phrase, a title, even a sketch of a melody. It'll help keep your creativity flowing.

Sometimes my reward is a day off to visit the Van Gogh exhibit, a bouquet of flowers, an Envy apple, or when nobody's looking, a party-size bag of York Peppermint Patties.

NURTURING ASSIGNMENT

I want you to do something nice for yourself as a reward for all of your hard work. This could be the most important step in the creative process. Maybe you crave ice cream. Everybody's different. Do what makes you happy and is still within the law.

Whatever you do, make a point of acknowledging that you're doing it as a reward for what you've just created. It is a victory in itself, just because you did it, not because your song was downloaded ten million times. The victory starts with you.

KILL YOUR CRITIC

Sometimes, especially when we feel a little stuck, our critics arrive with an armada of hate. Their mission is to squash us.

This is how I deal with those monsters.

I assign them a physical form. Maybe it's a set of keys. Before I start working on a song, those keys go into a drawer, which I slam shut and lock. Tight. If, while I'm writing, that nasty beast seems to escape and belittle me, I unlock that drawer, scream "SHUT UP," relock the drawer, and whack the thought of that critic with a fly swatter. A lot.

If I still hear her yelling despicable things about my songs, I shove a tomato into a Ziploc bag and stomp it to death. While I'm doing that, I scream at her: "Go away, dammit. I'm writing. Get outta here. I'm working. I have beautiful things to say. Neither you nor anyone else has the right to stop me from doing my best work. Shut up, shut up, shut up. GET OUT!"

I buy lots of tomatoes.

When they're all squished to death, I feel like I have control of the situation instead of being a victim to that hideous voice.

On the rare occasion when the tomato puree stomp fails, I jump into the shower, turn on the pulsing hot water, and scream obscenities for twenty minutes. My throat is usually sore afterward, but at least I'm able to purge the critic from my soul.

I suggest you try some version of those activities next time your critic tells you to deep six songwriting and enroll at Tootsie's Law School over the 7-Eleven.

You ARE a songwriter. We need your words and music. Keep going.

You'll be glad you did. So will everyone else when we're all singing along with you at the Grammys.

DETERMINATION

Interview with Grammy-Winning Songwriter Debbie Hupp

If you don't know what chutzpah means, look up Debbie Hupp.

We were Facebook friends long before I knew she was a songwriter. She posted mouthwatering pictures of her southern cuisine along with the recipes. When I realized she'd written some of my favorite songs, I immediately asked for, and got, this interview.

An unhappy Kentucky housewife and mother of two, Debbie had written some poems that saw a little local success in Louisville. One day, while vacuuming her living room, she had to unplug the vacuum to get to the next room when she heard Johnny Cash singing "A Boy Named Sue" on TV. She said to herself, "I can do that."

She put some ideas down and called in some amateur musicians.

"They liked what I had written, and recorded my songs on an old reel-to-reel recorder in an empty room with good echo that used to house a furnace.

"From there, my plan was to watch Johnny Cash's next show, stay for the credits, and find his publisher, The House of Ash, in Hendersonville, Tennessee. Shocked that someone answered when I called, and even more stunned when nobody hung up on me, I spoke with Reba, Johnny's sister. She was cordial and made an appointment with me for Larry Lee to listen to five of my songs.

"I'd never been out of Kentucky before, but I drove myself up to meet with Larry Lee, Cash's song plugger. Thinking the meeting would be in a stern, corporate setting, I was surprised the office was an old house with railroad tracks behind it.

"Larry wasn't there yet and I was told to take a seat. Hours went by. I kept asking where he was and was adamant that I deserved to be seen. When he finally showed up, Larry was very nice, but swung his chair around so I couldn't see his face while he listened to my songs. When the music stopped, he played my tunes again. And again.

"'I'll take this song and this song,' he said. One was 'Golden Haired Angel.' 'I can't take the others. They're too pop. But I tell you what you might wanna do.'

"He wrote down the address for Screen Gems Columbia, and called ahead to tell Johnny MacRae I was coming.

"Johnny MacRae listened but he didn't think he could use these songs. However, he wanted me to go home, continue to write, and send him everything.

"I had wings to fly back to Louisville."

Then life got in the way.

"I wrote a few songs, remarried, didn't take my writing seriously. To me, it was just an adventure. Eight years later, my husband went with me to see Johnny MacRae again, who was then at Combine. He told my husband this: 'I don't know what you have to do to keep her writing songs, but do it.'

"I didn't write melodies. I sang to the person who was putting my songs down. So MacRae introduced me to Bob Morrison, who'd co-written 'Looking for Love in All the Wrong Places' and 'Love the World Away.'

"Together, we wrote some strong songs right out of the gate. And Larry Butler, Dotty West's producer, held one of them for her for over a year. Then another of his artists went through Dotty's stack of holds, found our song, and said, 'Don't give it to her. I want it.'

"He got it. Our song was 'You Decorated My Life.' Kenny Rogers was the artist, and his recording, which was on his *Lucille* album, went to number one, and we won a Grammy!

"Meanwhile, I had five kids in Louisville, where my husband wasn't doing much to help support them. It fell to me. So, no matter how well my songs were doing, I always had a day job. One of them was at night, guarding Seagram's, where their whiskey was stored. I walked around the grounds singing new ideas into my tape recorder.

"Back in Nashville, Johnny MacRae was always nice to me and wanted me to continue bringing him my new songs. That was flattering, but I was learning the music business, and wouldn't leave his office without a contract.

"He finally gave in, but my contract with Combine did not include a weekly advance. Even so, we had a hot song plugger—Al Cooley.

With his help, I had four more number ones: 'Are You on the Road to Loving Me Again' (Debby Boone), 'Don't Call Him a Cowboy' (Conway Twitty), 'A Straight Tequila Night' (John Anderson), and, of course, 'You Decorated My Life' (Kenny Rogers).

"I would've been rich if I hadn't raised five kids pretty much on my own. But I love them and would do it all over. With my royalties, I bought a house in Kentucky. Unlike most writers who hope to live on their songwriter income, I always had a job. One was a business I owned, as a uniformed security officer.

"I hear a song in everything. I'm very observant of tones of voices, facial expressions. Sometimes it's worth putting into a song. 'You Decorated My Life' was written for my children. I'm so proud of who they are.

"I was persistent. I guess I was lucky, compared to the odds of me and someone else. I just keep doing it. I am still writing with new, young writers."

Debbie is a good, smart, articulate, enlightened lady, and a righteous babe. Listen to her new songs, and try her lemon meringue pie.

CHAPTER 2
HOW TO WRITE A HIT MELODY

A melody is a series of single notes with rhythm. It's what we sing, whistle, and hum. It is definitely not a chord progression.

When composing a tune, I tap out the rhythm on my knee, then pick out the individual notes on my keyboard with my right hand, while my left hand stays behind my back. Lefty aches to play chords, but knows I'll get to them later.

While composing, I make a point of saving every draft. You never know which one will fly.

I urge you to save everything. Immediately. Don't ever trust yourself to remember your ideas, swearing you'll write them down later. There is no later. When you're about to fall asleep, and a life-changing idea pops into your head, don't groan and say you'll deal with it in the morning. The chances are 100 percent to less than nothin' you won't remember what seemed good the night before. And you'll hate yourself for being cavalier about letting it go.

Ideas are fragile and ultra-sensitive. If you ignore them, they'll float into someone else's head. Later, when their song is number one on the *Billboard* chart, you'll scream, "Hey, that's my song!" No, it *could've* been, but you didn't honor it.

I always start with the chorus. Let's suppose you have a cool melody with a surprising rhythm for that section. Then I want you to use the same one-note-at-a-time process to find just the right notes and rhythm for your verse. Again, no chords yet. They're comin'. I promise.

Now you've got your verse and chorus rhythms and melodies, which, ideally, are different from each other, but in the same tempo. At this point, you're two thirds of the way home.

See? Easy.

Now you need a third section for your song.

The final section in writing a song is called a bridge. This simply connects the chorus to the last chorus and gives the lyric a place to say what it hasn't already said, on top of a rhythm that's different from the ones in your other two sections. Be comforted in knowing there is no one I've met in my entire songwriting life, on this or any other planet, who likes writing bridges.

"Couldn't I just repeat the chorus?"

"No."

"But my chorus is so strong, wouldn't a bridge be anti-climactic?

"Nope. Not if it's a good bridge."

"But..."

"Xillary, write your bridge."

I have this conversation with my clients twenty times a week. But I tell them it's better to have a good bridge and take it out later if the track is too long than need one at three in the morning when THE CALL comes from someone representing a project you desperately want. It's unlikely you'll be able to come up with a strong bridge on the spot. If you don't use that section for song A, you'll always have it in reserve for song D, later.

A colleague, who evolved from writing hits to becoming a music publishing executive at a major movie studio, sums up bridge work this way: "When I die, if by some miracle I get into Heaven, it will be on the condition that God wants me to rewrite the bridge first."

Ideally, the rhythm and individual melody notes in the bridge section are different from those in the verse and chorus. To simplify the process, I start by tapping a rhythm on my knee, making silly sounds like ooh gooba gooba booba baby baby ooh.

Once I have an unpredictable rhythm, which fits with the verse and chorus melody and rhythm, then, and only then, I hold auditions for the chords.

See? I told you we'd get there.

CHOOSE THE INDIVIDUAL NOTES FIRST

If you write the chords first, your individual melody notes have to be squished inside the chord. That's very limiting. However, by writing the notes first, your melody can go anywhere sing-able (which, for most artists is an octave and three). When it gets there, you have many more possibilities to surround your notes with the chords you **want,** not just the ones you're stuck with.

Some tunesmiths swear by sitting at their keyboards, wailing away on them, crankin' their chord progressions, at ninety DB. If that works for you and you're on the charts, livin' the dream, fine, keep going. But if you're not there yet, try it this way.

Just try it.

Using the amazing software we have on our laptops and phones can transform a simple tune like "Twinkle, Twinkle Little Star" into sounding like it's been recorded by a seventy-piece orchestra. I'm all for that. But first, please start with your simple melody, with rhythm, then chords, before you start adding the didgeridoos.

In constructing a commercial melody, there are several guidelines to follow.

DURATION

Most hit songs are somewhere around thirty-two bars long.

At one time, all songs had to have thirty-two bars. Period. End of discussion. But now, some have thirty-one bars, some thirty-three, some fifty and a half, because while they follow the **guidelines** of form, they aren't stuck in it. Music *is* an art after all. But no matter how many bars you have in your song, ideally, you should get to your hook, or chorus, in somewhere around twenty-five or thirty seconds, unless your rhythm is surprisingly delicious and totally warrants more time. Same with the chorus.

YOU ONLY HAVE SIX SECONDS

At a recent ASCAP expo, I was in the room where a panel of music supervisors, looking for new material for their projects, was listening to song pitches. These are the people with almost total control over what music goes into TV shows, movies, video games, and commercials.

There were fifty hopeful songwriters and singer/songwriters in the room, and the panelists, many of whom I know to be supportive and gracious, listened to each track for six seconds. Only six seconds. If the writer/artist didn't grab them by then, the panelists passed. Some of them actually tossed CDs into the air like Frisbees, heading for the trash.

That is how it is. You want to be in the music business? This is what y'got. Leikin's first law is give 'em what they want. Don't dumb down your gifts. Just present them in an easily marketable way so the executive on the other side of the desk can say yes.

In view of this, I want you to keep the intros to your songs short. Don't blow your shot at life-changing ears by going on too long. Nobody is going to **wait** for something to happen. **Make** it happen right away.

Jingles do that. Pay attention to them. Listen. They're all over your media. Jingles last ten, fifteen, or thirty seconds. In, out, end. Fifteen seconds. There's no warmup or intro. They're all hook. Boom. Note one—here it is.

I keep hearing "Liberty, Liberty, Li-berty," the jingle for Liberty Mutual. There's no warm-up at all. From note one it's all hook. Same with "Plop Fizz Fizz," the Alka Seltzer jingle. And State Farm's "Like a Good Neighbor, State Farm is There."

JINGLE EXERCISE

For fun, write three jingles, even with nonsense words: one for Coca-Cola, one for a website selling beauty products, and another for saving the planet. (Be aware you can't use your jingles for those products down the road without the company's permission.)

Now, back to the tune. After the title, the melody is the most important part of the song. Lyricists might be upset hearing this, but it is the truth. Make peace with it. The tune is the first thing we hear. If we like it, we'll stay with it and respond in a very open, natural, subjective state—like toddlers. I love watching them when music is playing. They wiggle and jiggle. If they don't, you haven't done your job as a songwriter.

When we hear a new song, we either like it immediately or we don't. If we do, it usually isn't until we've heard it four or five times that we ever hear the words. On the other hand, you can write a devastating, brilliant lyric, but if the melody doesn't get us, sadly, nobody will ever hear what you wrote.

The function of the melody is to reach out and grab us in an unguarded, primitive, totally emotional state, and hold our attention long enough for the lyric to take hold and give us some words so we can sing along. But the lyric can't do the melody's job. The tune and rhythm drive a composition. Then the lyric steps in and brings it all home.

Whatever you create melodically, lyrically, and rhythmically, keep your audience surprised. If your song becomes predictable, you'll lose 'em. Once they go, they're gone. Remember, you need magic in your tunes. You're not creating music by the pound.

Do I write a ballad or an uptempo song?

As much as I love ballads, and ache to write more, the reality is that most songs on the charts these days are uptempo. They have big, singalongable choruses, and when they start, all bets are off. You can't help but sing along. For proof, listen to the top forty pop and new country songs on the *Billboard* chart in your genre every week.

I make a two-hour drive, each way, at least once a month. It's pretty, with the Pacific Ocean on my right, but I need my music in the passenger seat. I did that route yesterday and tuned in to our new country station. For four solid hours, it was uptempo tracks all the way. Not a single ballad.

Leikin's law: Give 'em what they want.

If that's tough for you, write one for you, one for the media.

RANGE

The suggested range of a pop song is usually an octave and three. For example, from middle C to the C one octave above it, to the E a few notes above the second C. Most singers in the pop and new country genres can manage that range. But I shudder to tell you many of my early songs exceeded it and weren't recorded because of that. Back in the day, when I was just starting my career, and Sinatra was cutting, Ole Blue Eyes couldn't hit the high note in "You Set My Dreams to Music," which I wrote with

Steve Dorff. Steve and I have had more than a hundred recordings of that tune, but it sure would've been nice to count Sinatra's version as one of them.

The same thing happened with "An American Hymn." My writing partner wrote the score for *East of Eden*, and Milt Okun, his mentor, wanted a lyric for the main theme. I wrote it, all the while begging my co-writer to trim the range from an octave and five to octave and three. Fifteen years later, when Celine Dion was interested in recording "An American Hymn," my writing partner finally trimmed the range to an octave and three.

However, during those fifteen years, two hundred artists tried, but failed, to sing our song. We don't *get* those offers very often. When you do, keep them singable.

Most people are more comfortable writing lyrics than music because we speak words and write words. We use them constantly, so we get to practice daily.

But we don't speak music. That's okay. Music is something we feel, something we hear inside our heads and in our hearts. And there isn't a nanosecond of our lives when we don't feel something. So don't be intimidated by your iffy or missing musicianship, your inability to read notes, or even play an instrument. Many of the world's greatest musicians never write anything. They interpret what other people have already composed. Don't feel you have to be a great keyboard player or guitarist to write a tune, or that being a virtuoso cellist means you can compose equally great melodies.

During one six-month period, three of my clients were prodigies from Julliard. They had awards and citations and plaques and scholarships for performing and interpreting Brahms and the rest of those guys. But between them, nobody could create an original, commercial melody. Therefore, I'd rather hear your timid beginnings, a cappella, than the pompous stylings of a tuba hero who thinks pop songs are piffle.

When I get an assignment to write an original song, I turn on my app and always start with the melody, choosing one note at a time. Although I have limited chops as a keyboard player, I *do* hear melodies or parts of melodies in my head, and feel contagious, irresistible rhythms, tapping them on my knee. I keep my recording app on, in my car, my purse, on my guest pillow, in my pocket, even in the shower. That way, whenever I get an idea, I just hum it into the app. Sometimes I call my voicemail and sing to myself. Constantly revising, I go over and over and over what I've started, saving every draft. Y'never know.

You may work differently, and if that's getting you where you want to be on the charts, great. But remember, songwriting is a process, and often, what comes out in a burst of unbridled creativity is a first draft, not a finished, market-ready tune. It usually needs several more versions to be as strong as it needs to be in order to realistically compete in the marketplace. I'm lucky because as I'm working, I feel a little click in my gut when I'm pretty sure what I'm writing is finished. But I'm still not adding chords. I add them last.

When I write on assignment, I already know the artist, genre, and feel. If you aren't an artist writing for yourself, choose one on a chart in your genre and do the same thing I do. If you're a singer/songwriter, pretend you don't sing, and as an exercise, follow my suggestions. This isn't forever. It's a "for now." Deal?

From consulting with so many talented, developing writers, I discovered they often start with too many chords, no melody, way too much technology, and not enough bare bones note-by-note creativity. If you find your melodies aren't as strong as you would like them to be, or the marketplace demands, then I suggest you try some version of my process and adapt it to your personality.

When you change the process, you can change the result.

For most songwriters, composing music is not a matter of deciding about quarter notes and staccato sixteenths and minor thirds. Having some music "chops" would certainly help you create strong melodies, but it isn't mandatory. If you hear a tune inside your head, you can whistle or hum it into a recording app on your phone and then hire an arranger to embellish it with chords.

Remember: a melody is a series of single notes, with rhythm, that you can hum, whistle, or sing in the shower. No chords necessary in its conception. You can add the band later.

When I'm commissioned to write a new song, I always start with the melody. As stated earlier, my left hand is behind my back while I sit at my keyboard. With my right hand, I choose one note at a time. NO CHORDS. With my recording app on, I don't settle for the first idea. I keep on rolling.

Y'never know what series of notes or rhythm pattern is going to show up. So please, please, remember to record everything. Always. Don't think you'll remember it later. You won't. Even if your Pizza Delivery Specialist is ringing your doorbell, or a water pipe bursts, don't ever leave a hot keyboard when you're on a roll.

GATHERING IDEAS

Sometimes, my best ideas come when I'm doing something else. Today, when I began my morning routine, I opened the blinds and looked for my *L.A. Times* on the driveway. I noticed it wasn't there. Again. Half asleep, I said, it's too early for the paper boy. WHOA! A bell rang in my head. Hey, that's a great opening line for a song.

I never get the whole song in one sitting.

It would be excellent if songs came to us whole. But most of the time, they don't. So please beware of thinking a first inspiration draft is a finished song. It's an early draft.

Yes, there are stories about Ditzy Scnitzy writing "You need more fiber in your diet" in ten seconds and winning a Grammy. That's the exception. It's not productive to spend time looking up other songs that are hits that arrived as quickly. There's no award for speed. Only quality.

Don't ever tell someone you wrote a song in ten minutes. It usually signals an unfinished work. On the other hand, telling the same person you worked on a song for three years isn't much of a calling card either. So, leave the time elements out of your pitches.

Songs usually come to us a little at a time—a few notes here, a little rhythm there. It's frustrating. Often, there's one line, or even one word, I can't get for weeks. I obsess over it. I repeat the other lines over and over in the shower, on the rare occasion when I'm sweeping the floors, or while stuck on the 101 behind a tomato truck sharing its cargo with the road in front of me. The note or word I need might pop into my head while I'm chopping an apple, watering my succulent garden, or organizing my t-shirt collection by color and birthdate. And 99.999 percent of the time, the missing syllable appears when I'm not actually at the keyboard.

I truly believe if I got the first part, the rest is in there somewhere. It'll come when it's ready.

THE SUBCONSIOUS NEVER STOPS WORKING

Here's my playful take on how it functions.

Let's say your subconscious is a one-hundred-floor library. It goes down into the earth another hundred floors. At the front desk, you ring a bell for your personal librarian. She asks, "What do you need today, Miss Molly?"

"The word for the last line of my chorus to 'Thank God for York Peppermint Patties.'"

"Thank you. I'll notify you when it's ready."

My librarian gathers her entire staff and shares what I need. They disperse like Energizer bunnies to the endless reference sections all over the enormous edifice that is my subconscious. Red books. Blue books. Green newspapers. Fiction. Nonfiction, sci fi. Young adult fiction. Nursery rhymes.

I leave the library and go home to bake my sour cream cinnamon-raisin coffee cake, nuts optional. Maybe I floss, or toss frayed t-shirts in the Goodwill bag, buy Envy apples at Trader Joe's, or fill up at the good Chevron station. And when I'm not screaming "I need that line! That one line! C'mon!" the bell at the front desk of my subconscious library dings, and the idea I've been searching for floats in.

I trust my imagination and my subconscious. They've never, ever let me down. I start my morning by stretching under the giant Sycamore tree shading the patio. Then, turning on the classical channel and having my first cup of tea, I do the crossword puzzle, listening to Tchaikovsky, Rachmaninov, Mozart etc. Last week, I wondered how it must have felt to Beethoven, in Vienna, in 1801, sipping a goblet of red wine, working at his grand piano and realizing when his composition was finished: "Gott—ich habe gerade die Mondscheinsonate geschrieben!" God, I just wrote the Moonlight Sonata!

TWEAKING PREDICTABLE MELODIES

When new clients come to me with promising songs, they often play predictable melodies, with the same predictable rhythm, and ask for my input on which chord progressions will make their compositions more interesting. If you get yourself into a hole melodically, it's often because you're relying on the **chords** to do the **melody's** job. They can't.

You don't hum chords. But you do whistle tunes.

Contrary to what you've seen romanticized in movies, most contemporary writers do not write their songs on staff paper while composing. Like a majority of tunesmiths, they use their recording apps. Once their tune is finished, then they may jot the notes on staff paper, and/or use software like Sibelius to do it for them. However, the truth is, almost nobody in the songwriting business reads or writes music. They listen.

Just as each lyrical phrase should relate to the title, every musical phrase should also fit the music of the title line. Ideally, it all belongs in the same song. For example, the chorus of "Righteous Slime" wouldn't fit with "Ave Maria."

MELODY EXERCISE

Write a new melody to the lyric of "God Moves the Pen."

You have a new, well-constructed set of words to use as your guide. Put one note of music on each syllable of the lyric. Make sure, as you sing the new song, that you stress the words as you would when speaking them. Don't put the em-**pha**-sis on the wrong syl-**lable**.

However, you have a lot of freedom to change the rhythm of the verses to 3/4, 5/8, 2/2, 7/11, or whatever you like. Nothing has to be the same as it is in the original melody except the form. Verse/chorus, verse/chorus. For once in your life, a bridge is optional—for your first few practice songs. One major "should," though: go *up* into your chorus. The interval I recommend is a major third—for example, from the note C to the note C an octave above it, to the note E a few steps up from there. And notice I said note, not chord.

Sometimes, if your chorus rhythm is so completely surprising and whomps you on note one of that section, you can get away without going up. But tension builds as you go up the scale and the little hairs on the back of your neck do too. Don't lose that tension by going down the scale, or sideways, instead of up. Most of the time, if you don't have a startling rhythmic change at the beginning of your chorus, heading down the scale is like letting air out of a balloon.

I also strongly suggest you keep your song in the same key until you modulate up half a step from the last note of the bridge into the final chorus. Usually, changing keys after the verse, into the chorus, is a sign that the melody is weak. I don't want you to waste a beautiful verse melody, and especially a chorus, on a bad interval. Deal?

SOFTWARE

I love it. Most of my songwriting colleagues, plus the producers who record my songs, do too. Every year, there's a newer version. Even better. Most prefer Pro Tools. Whatever makes my team happy makes me happy as well.

But before you start recording anything, know this: it all starts with a good song. From day one I've been saying, "You can't fix it in the studio," and it's still true. Once you've got a song with a melody you can't stop singing, with an irresistibly singa-longable chorus, THEN open your software and bring it home.

All of the suggestions I offer you are ones I use, as do my successful clients. Cartoonist Scott Adams said, "Creativity is allowing yourself to make mistakes. Art is knowing which ones to keep."

INSPIRATION

After music, visual art is my biggest passion. I constantly visit museums like LACMA, MOCA, and the Hammer Museum in Los Angeles. No matter how bizarre, I am slurped up by the music on the walls. (Steve Dorff and I already wrote this one.) Since I live in Santa Barbara, I spend the day driving there, letting my eyes dance for my entire Art Day, and then race home across the sunset over my Pacific Ocean.

When I was a student hitchhiking across Europe, I travelled with two art majors. We visited every museum, gallery, and pile of rocks (oops—excavation) in every country. Although I groaned when touring Pompei, as a result of visiting every museum in Europe and seeing everything firsthand, I grew to need art in my life as much as I need music.

Before that student adventure, I couldn't understand how Cézanne's Card Players could be in the Musée d'Orsay when it hung over my aunt's fireplace in frozen Canada. Imagine being that naïve? Well, I was.

But I learned quickly. Any opening of any art show or museum gala, I'm there. So I was particularly passionate about seeing Andy Warhol's Campbell's Soup Cans, all in one place for the first time since they were painted, at the Museum of Contemporary Art in downtown Los Angeles.

While visiting, I snapped photos of all twenty-three varieties of the artist's Campbell's Soup Cans. And I was elated. However, I was strongly "encouraged" by a seven-foot security guard who, as we say in California, was out of alignment with his higher, best self, to delete all of my pictures, and exit immediately.

Oh?

On my way home, I stopped at a market and bought all twenty-three varieties of Campbell's soup. To this day, those cans sit on my coffee table. When visitors ask why I haven't put away my groceries, I tell them that's my latest acquisition and ask them to please not touch my art collection.

Then I wrote the song "Gum and String and Starlight" with Steve Dorff. This is proof that one art stimulates another.

In art, as well as music, it's always about the surprises.

IS YOUR WORK ORIGINAL?

With so much music being created these days, and with such great access to it everywhere we go, it's easy to "borrow" someone else's melody without realizing it.

When I'm worried about that, I run my new tune by a few colleagues. Sometimes I can fix it by adding another note, taking one out, or changing the rhythm. But if I can't, I start fresh with a new tune. It's devastating. But as a pro, I know it has to be done.

One of our responsibilities as songwriters is to be thoroughly knowledgeable of every song on every platform. It sounds like an overwhelming task. But it's your job to be aware of what other people have already written so you don't duplicate or infringe on someone else's intellectual property.

Believe me, you don't want to become the defendant in an infringement trial. The owner of the copyright of the original song from which you "borrowed," intentionally or not, always wins.

SONG FIRST, VIDEO LATER

Videos are usually works of art. I love 'em. Everybody loves them.

However, write your song first. We'll hear it before we see it. And as much as we all crave music, few of us make listening to it a primary occasion. We're usually doing something else, too, like washing dishes, driving, grocery shopping, dusting, gardening, scooting to class, doing laundry, or shopping for Johnny Was leggings on sale. We usually don't see the video first. Our initial connection is not visual. We hear it.

So when you know your finished song is righteous, and you've run it by colleagues, and/or a consultant first, to make sure what you **think** you've got is really **what** you've got, **then** move on to your video. I know that's not what you long to hear, but it's the truth.

Ninety percent of your initial effort should be spent writing your song. Period. If it's not a strong, original tune to begin with, nothing's going to save it.

I know that's not what you want to hear. But it's the truth.

MELODY TO A LYRIC EXERCISE

Write a note-by-note melody, no chords, to the lyric of any song you like.

I can't say this often enough. A melody is a series of single notes, with rhythm. It's not a bunch of gnarly sounds or riffs you found in your software. That's a track, not a tune. A melody is what you sing *over* the track. It's what you whistle, what you hum, what you play with one finger on your keyboard.

In addition to making your heart happy and writing the truth, if you're looking for commercial success, your job is to make it easy for the people on the other side of the desk to say yes. Most of them are fearful of holding onto their jobs and are in the business of saying no. So, again, make it easy for them to tell you what you want to hear.

Because of software, it's easy for songwriters to fall into what I call the "technical toy trap." That's when you rely on your software to do your composing for you. To avoid that pitfall, try to hear the melody in your head first. Don't just play or strum chords and wait for the notes to appear between them. HEAR the music in your head. Once you write the simple melody and rhythmic line, then, of course, go to your instrument to embellish. But don't rely on software to do your initial creating for you. Trust your gut, and your heart, to tell you what you're feeling and what needs to be translated into a melody. Then, go to your software.

THE GUITAR

I love that instrument. I can play awesome rhythms on it. Nothing is more fun or intimate than holding it close, strumming, and singing along. After all these years, I still cherish my baritone ukulele. However, most guitar players play rhythm only and don't pick out individual notes. They end up playing chord progressions while the individual notes of the melody are forced to be inside the chords you're using. But if you choose the individual notes first, there will be more chords to go with them. Then, of course, after you know your notes, I urge you to go back to your guitars.

As a result, when writing a new song, I use a guitar and a keyboard.

What, you ask? What? Is she nuts? My answer is, try it. If you hate it, absolutely despise it, and you're where you want to be in your career now, don't do it again. But please, if you're not there yet, and what you've been doing isn't working, give it a shot. My Grammy-winning clients do this. You can too.

WRITING INSTRUMENTALS

Some talented clients who don't write lyrics, and are intimidated by them, tell me they only write instrumentals, and simply don't deal with words. They insist their compositions don't need them. Fine, sign up with a music library or pitch those tracks for syndicated how-to TV shows. But those are long odds. Very long odds. These same writers also cite the one lonely instrumental per year that makes it onto the charts.

Then I point out that every vocalist and band needs whole songs, with words, to sing. Therefore, melody-only recordings have the least chance of breaking through. I also recommend these talented instrumentalists find a strong lyric writer as a collaborator. Then they have twice the potential income streams.

As a consultant, I've put several teams together. Maybe someday soon, one of them will be yours. I hope so.

By now, you've written a brand-new verse/chorus, verse/ chorus lyric that is well structured. And you've written a brand-new melody to that excellent lyric of yours. Congratulations! You've just written what could well be your first hit! Celebrate!

I excel at this. For each finished song, I get myself a little gift. Sometimes, it's a perfect pink grapefruit. Or a bouquet of daffodils. A visit to an art museum. Yoga at the beach. A toast to the evening star. Whatever it is you do that makes you feel rewarded, tell yourself, out loud, good for me. I wrote a great song! And I deserve this! I really deserve this!

The more self-love, the more willing the five-year-old inside your heart will feel brave enough to come out and play again for your next tune.

The more you write, the better you get, the easier it is, and the more you have a shot at each new one being your first million-download.

JOINT WORK

If you write lyrics only or tunes only, you should be aware than once words are added to a preexisting tune, or a tune is added to a preexisting lyric, it becomes a joint work. From then on, even if that piece of music is played instrumentally, or the lyric is recited without music, unless previously stipulated in writing and drawn up by an entertainment attorney, the lyricist is co-author, and half-owner of the copyright. So is the composer.

When you collaborate, make absolutely sure you get everything in writing. Never assume you can trust anybody you're working with, especially a friend, relative, or lover. In this business of music, relationships without written documentation go south quickly, especially when there is a lot of money at stake.

Here's a terrible case study.

For twenty successful years, I collaborated with a composer who wrote gorgeous, soaring, goosebump tunes. We always split all royalties 50/50, and had agreements, signed by both of us, to confirm it.

Then along came Plácido Domingo, who wanted a lyric for one of my co-writers' TV themes. I wrote it. It's beautiful. Domingo recorded our song, we made some tasty mechanical royalties, and received platinum records from dozens of countries, which hang on my trophy wall.

However, as a result of exposure by the most famous tenor in the world at the time, Michelle Kwan (even now our greatest American ice skater, who won gold medals almost every time out) started using the instrumental in her short- and long-form programs. It was thrilling.

Nonetheless, although I searched for those performances on my royalty statements, apparently, this yutz I trusted for so long didn't file the song with my lyric as a joint work. He claimed I should only receive royalties when the song was sung.

That was news to me. All of our other songs created the same way were joint works. Why was this one an exception?

That disagreement destroyed our long, successful relationship. I never worked with him again. And I never got a farthing from those thousands of instrumental performances either. In the end, I chocked it up to my co-writer's fifth wife, or was it the sixth, who needed more shoes.

It was a hard lesson. Now, I don't trust anybody. I swear to you, if the Dalai Lama was in my kitchen drinking chamomile tea with me, and I had to excuse myself to go potty, I'd take my purse along.

I don't mean to ever insult anyone, especially the Dalai Lama, by that remark. But I do want you all to make sure your creations are joint works, with everything in ink, stating that. Please do it, just in case you write **your** "American Hymn" someday, and your gracious, spiritual co-writer transmogrifies into sewage before your eyes.

For the first couple of years after this incident, that guy sent emails suggesting we put this behind us, resume writing together, and why don't I meet him at Babalu on Montana, for dinner. Oh?

I replied this way: First, send me a certified check for $350,000. Then, sure, I'll meet you at Babalu, on Montana Avenue, right after my second slow dance with Hitler.

The music business can be scurrilous. Sometimes, even when you have signed agreements, a slimeball can decide not to pay you, and dodges you long enough for the statute of limitations to run out. This happened to me when a colleague representing lyricist Gene Lees wanted to sell his catalog of songs and was looking for a buyer. I introduced her to broker Owen Husney, with whom I had a signed and dated agreement, stating he'd pay me 20 percent of the selling price. But I never got a penny. He claimed he had cancer, and that my lawyer's calls were making him sicker.

I finally threw up my hands. Since then, I've trusted the universe to send me $20,000 for an assignment I'm not expecting. As for Owen, Karma will catch up with him.

Enjoy your creative process. Writing is supposed to be fun. Don't torture yourself. Creating takes time. Although it may take a day, a week, or a month, that's fine, because when something beautiful or catchy or both is finished, all you remember is the song, not the struggle. I'd rather have a half-finished tune that sparkles and promised to be special than a dozen completed songs that are iffy at best, sounding like everything else I've already heard, penned by other tunesmiths.

Be proud of yourself. Pamper yourself. As I said earlier, the more self-love, the more willing the five-year-old inside your heart will feel brave enough to come out and play again for your next tune.

The more you write, the better you get, the easier it is, and the more you have a shot at each new composition being your first million-download.

Keep going!

You can do it.

JUST KEEP WRITING

Q&A WITH GRAMMY NOMINEE JP SAXE

I'm always fascinated by the songs my clients like to listen to, especially when what they crave is from a new artist.

One Saturday morning, a very talented lady in Blue Hill, Maine was raving about JP Saxe. I immediately loved him. The hook to his song "If the World Was Ending," written with Julia Michaels, had me singing along instantly. Even the squirrels in my Sycamore tree were slow dancing to it.

After almost a year of trying to hook up with JP for an interview, since he was so slammed for time, we decided I would send him questions, and between red lights in the rush-hour Hollywood rain, he'd record his answers.

Molly Leikin: Who taught you to write songs?

JP Saxe: Micah Barnes was my mentor, in Toronto. At fourteen, I was obsessed with the Beatles Songbook and played every tune incessantly. I also loved Gershwin and his songbook.

ML: Who are your musical heroes?

JPS: Stevie Wonder, Paul Simon, Carol King.

ML: What's your writing process?

JPS: To warm up, I journal. I'm more sincere in my song when I'm not thinking about my feelings and thoughts being songs. When I'm stuck, I go back to journaling. Writer's block is a myth. It's being afraid of writing bad songs. Just keep writing. You'll get to the good ones.

ML: Who inspires you?

JPS: The poets I hang out with. Edwin Bodney, Alyesha Wise, Tonya Ingram, and Yesika Salgado.

ML: What inspires you?

JPS: I always write from my own experience, trying to get the feeling to match real life.

ML: Do you prefer writing alone or co-writing?

JPS: Writing feels like a conversation with me, or with someone else.

ML: What comes first? Music, rhythm, words?

JPS: Always words first—the rhythm and melodies are in the words.

ML: Who do you wish you could write with?

JPS: Maren Morris, Stevie Wonder.

ML: Where is your favorite place to write?

JPS: At my piano at 3 a.m.

ML: Is there something you always wear to write?

JPS: Bombas. I religiously purchase *Shark Tank* products.

ML: Which songs do you wish you had written?

JPS: "Maybe I'm Amazed." "Somewhere Over the Rainbow."

ML: What is your favorite music now?

JPS: Depends on the day. *Channel Orange*, Jamie Cullum, Oscar Peterson, Alabama Shakes (last album).

ML: What is your favorite music of all time?

JPS: *Tapestry* (Carole King), Keith Jarrett, *Blue* (Joni Mitchell).

ML: What haven't you done yet that you'd like to do?

JPS: I'd like to tour South America. I wanna be on *Celebrity Jeopardy!*

ML: What would you like to be doing in twenty years?

JPS: I wanna be kicking it with my elementary school–age kids and jamming with them in a tricked-out tour van in Greece.

ML: What advice do you have for new writers?

JPS: Ask, "How can I be myself better?" Don't be afraid of writing bad songs. If you write a bad song, don't identify with that. Keep writing and the good ones will come to you.

ML: If you weren't doing music, what would you be doing instead?

JPS: I'd be captain of the Canadian bowling team.

ML: Do you believe in being in love forever?

JPS: Yes, but I'm bad at it.

Eight days after our interview, JP Saxe and Julia Michaels's song, "If the World Was Ending," was nominated for a Grammy. It's on YouTube.

CHAPTER 3

RHYMING

Ideally, good songs say something new. They are feelings, situations, and stories that we haven't heard before, set to music. Rhyming makes them accessible, singalongable, and memorable.

Children love nursery rhymes, and they easily remember them because of the repetitive sounds and rhythm. There's a playful child in the personality of every adult, too, so we can also be reached easily through rhyme, rhythm, and repetition.

The choruses of most songs are nursery rhymes for adults.

Fine, but you may ask yourself, why should you stress and go without sleep for days trying to make your lyrics rhyme and say something unique when all you hear are recycled, ordinary lyrics and sloppy rhymes? I'll answer by saying you've chosen the wrong examples. There are many songs now that **do** say something extraordinary in a passionate way and rhyme at the same time. But many songwriters have chosen near rhymes, or rhyme sounds, like love and truck.

That's not what I do or suggest to my clients who are learning the craft of lyric writing, but as of this writing, near rhymes are all over the charts.

Nonetheless, I feel it's important to learn the rules of rhyming, if only to know how to break them.

WHAT IS A RHYME?

A perfect rhyme is May, way, hey, gray. An imperfect rhyme is day, ways, grayed. Nobody will ever NOT record a song with near or slant rhymes, but lyric writing is a craft, and rhyming is part of that craft. It's more a matter of tradition and pride on the part of the writer.

I always strive for perfect rhymes in my own work and often drive my collaborators berserk with my meticulousness. However, I think my songs are stronger as a result. It took me a long time before I could accept a near or bastard rhyme like home and alone. Rhyming can make a good song better. But obviously it's more important to choose words that mean something and say something in a new, imaginative way than merely making the words rhyme for the sake of rhyming.

All good lyricists feel they should go for the perfect rhyme over the imperfect one but agree it's better to say something scintillating that doesn't rhyme perfectly than just say something ordinary that doesn't. My guess is that if Hal David of Bacharach/David came down from rock 'n' roll Heaven today and tuned into a pop or new country station, he'd be upset with all the near rhymes. At the same time, he would probably be intrigued with the new vocabulary writers are using, plus all the new ways of conveying feelings, ideas, and emotions.

As an artist I shouldn't impose my values on you. I will only say that lyric writing is a craft, and rhyming is part of that craft.

The song "Live Like You Were Dying," which was an enormous hit for Tim McGraw (number one for ten weeks) uses some unusual rhymes. You can hear it on YouTube. Some rhymes are perfect, some aren't. But they include X-rays and next days, which to my knowledge, had never appeared in a hit pop/country song before. Kudos to Tim Nicholls and Craig Wiseman for reaching and stretching and going for something new.

Any good lyricist will forgive an imperfect rhyme in favor of a great story and an intensely emotional situation like this one in which the singer met someone who was diagnosed with cancer and was told by his doctor to live every day to the fullest. With that advice, he went skydiving, climbed the Rocky Mountains, rode a bull, loved more completely, was nicer to people, forgave them, and made absolutely every second count, which is something we should all do anyway, isn't it? He became a better husband, a better friend, he made time to go fishing, and he even read the Bible.

Another song I love and which made me scream with joyful triumph the first, and every time, I heard it, is called "Before He Cheats." It was a monstrous hit for Carrie Underwood and number one for five weeks. I kept telling my music publisher I wanted to meet the women who wrote that song. Turns out the writers were two men: Chris Tompkins and Josh Kear. They sure nailed the female POV.

Yes, they used a lot of near rhymes, but they also included some fabulous pictures, making this song and its story of heartbreak and retribution feel like a movie. The vocabulary is original and passionate. So we forgive the slant rhymes when the singer finds out her boyfriend has been cheating on her with a bleached-blonde tramp. The singer carved her initials into his new leather seats, takes a baseball bat—a Louisville slugger to be exact—to both headlights, and slashes all of his tires. (There's a woman after my own heart!) But hey—I'm not suggesting you all run out and wreck your exes' vehicles, but because this song is so unleashed and visual, we overlook the near rhymes and see ourselves vicariously getting even. The fantasy makes it fun to listen to and is as gratifying as the last scene in the movie *Crash*, where that nasty HMO clerk gets rear-ended on Christmas Eve.

This is and always will be an extraordinarily passionate, visual, and singalongable song. The original pictures make it fun to sing and easy to remember. Same with "God Moves the Pen," sung by Tim McGraw.

RHYMING PLACES

Most writers make their songs rhyme at the end of the line. Audiences expect them there. But in an attempt to surprise and entertain the listener, you might try moving the rhymes around. Instead of writing "I wish there was a boy for me/tall and cute as he can be," try this: "I wish there was a boy for me/he'd be cute and extremely tall." This way, the internal **e** sound carries through the line and makes that sound connect the lyric in places we don't expect. It also jogs the rhythm into being less expected.

Predictability is the death of art.

Remember, your job as a writer is to surprise your audience. Don't give them what they are expecting or they'll yawn and disappear.

AVOID OBVIOUS RHYMES

Love is a word I stay away from rhyming. When it's in a lyric, we know that "shove," "turtle dove," "glove," and "of" are coming. So I use love in a non-rhyming place, like earlier in the line. An example is, "I will love you." That way, the rhyme sound is ooh. There are lots more of them compared with words that rhyme with love.

There are other rhymes I stay away from simply because they're so predictable. When you use "double," you know "trouble" and "bubble" are coming. However, if you precede them with an unexpected adjective, your audience will be surprised. For example, "sweet trouble" or "half a double" are way more interesting.

You'll notice that most of the words in our daily vocabulary don't sing. For example, "garbage disposal knob" isn't particularly mellifluous. Neither is "bank vault." The words that are generally considered most singalongable—love, heart, need, kiss, miss, touch, and hold—have been used to death. Your job as lyricist is to find new, underused vocabulary for your songs.

For example, "orange" doesn't rhyme with anything but it **does** sing. So instead of using a near rhyme, try the OR sound in the next line a couple of times to carry out the rhyme. "I gave him m**or**e oranges; he **nor**mally **or**dered m**or**e pears." See? This way you're able to use a word that sings, has color, is a picture that isn't used very much, and which, in fact, probably has been avoided because it doesn't rhyme perfectly with anything.

RHYMING DICTIONARY

I own a rhyming dictionary. I also have a thesaurus. Both of these reference books were Bat Mitzvah gifts. At the time I thought, *What?* Couldn't someone have given me another cashmere sweater set instead? I obviously wasn't thinking like a songwriter. Now, all these years later, I never sit down to work without both tattered volumes at my side. They're taped together, as a result of injuries sustained while being hurled across the room when they didn't offer me the words I badly needed. I may not even open either volume during the writing of a particular lyric, but I keep the rhyming dictionary and the thesaurus for support, just in case. And just in case happens a lot.

Some people claim that referring to a rhyming dictionary is cheating. I couldn't disagree more. What that book gives us is a long list of possible rhyme sounds that will either provide us with the word we need or steer us in the right direction. If we need an "ong" rhyme, it'll set our subconscious digging for it even when we turn our attention to other matters. Stephen Sondheim always had his rhyming dictionary open on his desk.

No matter how many hours I spend in my office, it's usually when I'm away from my writing—taking a walk, practicing yoga, tending my garden—that the word I **do** want pops into my head.

However, watch out for this: be careful you're not just rhyming to rhyme. Be sure you're saying what you want to say, be sure it sounds natural, like conversation. That's where the craft of lyric writing comes in.

MY RHYMING PROCESS

I always write the story of the song before I start writing the words. When creating a lyric, the last thing I do is write the lyric. As discussed in chapter one, first I write the bare bones of the story, the beginning, middle, and end, and answer the five Ws: who, where, what, when, why, plus how. Then, when I have the story down, along with an interesting title, the song seems to write itself. I don't start with needing a rhyme for a line when I don't know where the story is going.

In some lyrics, I purposely rhyme as little as possible. That way I'm free to say almost anything. And boy, that freedom feels good.

No matter what your position on rhyming happens to be, lyrics are dialogue for singers. As mentioned earlier, and I can't stress this often enough, as you write your song words, ask yourself these important questions:

1. Would I say this if I were talking to a friend on the phone?

2. If not, how would I say it?

3. Have I heard this before?

4. If so, could I make it a little different?

5. If not, could I write something else?

By answering these queries truthfully, you will raise the level of your lyric writing along with your chances for success in the marketplace.

Your job when creating a song is always to tell your audience something new. Whatever you do, don't recycle cliches. You're too good for that.

Here's one of my lyrics that makes me proud. I wrote it with Steve Lawford.

"Chocolate Chips and Quicksand"

Can't see you and not rip my clothes off
You can't call when I don't shake
You're delicious but so destructive
What a sensuous catastrophe we make
CHORUS:
First you're all over me—like a bad suit
Then you blow me off—like I'm some prostitute
Your kiss, your touch—are substances that should be banned
Melting me like chocolate chips, drowning me in quicksand.
Oh I crash after too much sugar
I'm wiped out from your extremes
And I hate who I have become now

Where in the world is my self esteem
CHORUS:
BRIDGE:
Baby I've been too lonely
Too long I guess
'Cause when I'm screaming no, no more no
more
It always comes out yes
CHORUS:

© Red Amaryllis Music songmd@songmd.com

Steve sent me some of his work for consultation, and the title was hiding in a verse. I was stunned by how strong it was and suggested we write a whole new song together. In verse one, we could have said "each extreme" instead of "your extremes" to make it rhyme perfectly, but truthfully, it was awkward and stilted, so we added an "s," making it sound the way we talk.

Here's another song with a lyric I'm proud to have written, this time with Sonya Watts.

"I'll Remember for Both of Us"

Ticket stub—in my old jeans—in the bag for
Goodwill
First date, Springsteen, ooh a fiery chill
I was poetry, you an engineer
Oreos for breakfast on the Malibu pier
CHORUS:
Do-oo-oo-oo-oo-oo-oo oo you remember
Those idyllic moments of me and you
If looking back is hard for you to do
Don't worry, we'll never turn to dust
I'll remember for both of us.

Little white ca-an-dles blessing our bed
You built a sailboat, and I baked cinnamon
bread
We hiked in Zion halfway past the sky
'Til the message came from San Jose and
y'kissed me good-bye
CHORUS 2:
Do-oo-oo-oo-oo-oo-oo oo you remember
All those golden moments of me and you
If looking back is hard for you to do
I promise we'll never turn to dust
I'll remember for both of us.
Bridge:
Our old VW was ye-el-low low and black
Got us to Mexico, through Canada and back
We lived above the flower shop next to the
train
Stuck plastic bags in ceiling leaks when-
ever it would rain
CHORUS 2:

© Red Amaryllis Music

Sonya and I are especially proud of all the pictures we incor-
porated in the lyric. The more images, the easier it is to remember.
You can hear this lyric, and see it, so it appeals to two senses.

We could still be looking for a perfect rhyme for "dust" that
says what needs to be said in our chorus, but we finally chose
"us," the near rhyme, because it says exactly what we needed
the chorus to say. It fit with our story.

Writing this song was the only way I could say goodbye
to my brilliant, creative, witty, clever Ed, when he died of

Alzheimer's. And although I know he's gone, I still expect him to open my front door, smiling, make himself an Alka Seltzer, and hold me for the rest of the day, night, and forever.

YOUTUBE

How lucky we are that almost any hit song we want to hear, with the lyric, is available on YouTube. When you go there, be sure to listen to some of my favorites: "One Margarita" and "God Moves the Pen." You'll be proud to own a pencil. Sometimes the lines rhyme. Sometimes they don't. But they sure are great tunes you can't stop singing. And that's what we're all here to create.

So shoot for a perfect rhyme, but first, say what you mean and feel. If there isn't a perfect rhyme, use a near one.

CHAPTER 4

THE IMPORTANCE OF A STRONG TITLE

My songs are my children. I would never name my daughter Mary. She'd be Monet.

I would never name my son Jerry. He'd be Jerusalem.

By the same token, nobody in my family is called I Love You, Baby Baby, or Ooh.

The title of a song is the world's immediate introduction to it. If a music publisher, artist, band, A&R person, label, publicist, or media outlet receives a thousand mp3s a minute, and 999 of them are called "Baby, Ooh," and one of them is "Gorgeous Torture," which do you think the listener will choose to play first? Yes, "Gorgeous Torture." This proves the importance of a song title.

Some tunes I had to listen to immediately when I saw their titles on the *Billboard* charts include:

"drivers license" by Olivia Rodrigo and Dan Nigro

"More Than my Hometown" by Morgan Wallen, Michael Hardy, Ernest Keith Smith, and Ryan Vojtesak

"Bandaid on a Bullet Hole" by Morgan Wallen, Matt Dragstrem, Chase McGill, and Josh Thompson

"Half of my Hometown" by Kelsea Ballerini, Ross Copperman, Nicolle Galyon, Shane McAnally, and Jimmy Robbins

"you should see me in a crown" by Finneas O'Connell and Billie Eilish

"Mr. Perfectly Fine" by Taylor Swift

Nobody's looking for, or singing, the same old, same old. Everybody who's getting somewhere is writing their fingerprint. Those should be your goals too.

For any song, in any genre, we see the title first. If we like it, we stay tuned. The businesspeople and decision makers on the other side of the desk give us six seconds. If we don't grab them by then, we're toast. And deleted.

Don't blow your shot with an iffy title.

A writer can get lucky with a song called "You," or "You 'n' Me," or "Ooh Ooh Ooh," but if you write lyrics only and you don't sing, I suggest you make sure your contribution to the song and the track is spectacular. The way I look at it, my name is going on my work. That's my fingerprint. My legacy. People who listen to music for a living know the difference between something that's okay and something that's brilliant and deserves to be heard. So dig a little deeper and find the part of yourself that's unique and looking to be expressed in a way that no one else has done before. You can do it. And you'll be glad you did.

Many of you will argue with me, claiming that anything with a popular artist's name on it will sell. That's correct to a point. But breakthrough songs aren't ordinary. Most good writers and singer/writers who are making a living from their craft are smart about marketing too. It may not be what you want to hear, but it's true. Songs have to be easily accessible to the public. Just remember this: people need a flashy headline before they'll commit to reading a newspaper or magazine. Your title is the headline. Give it to them.

No record company wants to risk its investment in a major artist on a boring title. Their corporate goal is to make money, not to promote esoteric art that sells three copies. They look for strong, original titles that will make the audience say "YES!" immediately.

I had one client who wrote lovely melodies but boring titles. As an exercise, I had him go through the brand names of all the products under his kitchen sink and in his pantry to see how many song ideas he came up with. For example, Formula 409 could be the number of a motel room in which a couple is trysting. It might also be an area code to which your phone call, secret or other-wise, is being made. I bet you never thought of that before.

Once, when the hot, arid winds were blowing in from the desert and making my Santa Monica lips very dry, I bought some-thing called Lip Therapy to keep them from chapping. I realized in the check-out line that the name of that tube of moisturizer would make a great title. I want you to be on the lookout for that kind of moment.

DIG FOR INSPIRATION EXERCISE

Go to the shelves under your sink and in your pantry. See how many brand names you can find that could be clever double entendre titles. Start with Vanish, Ultra Soft, matches. Marie Calendar could be a woman disguised as a man you secretly loved during the Civil War. Or you could play on her surname. This was the year Marie and I had together. Cinnamon might be the name of your truck. Or, when you sprinkle a little of that spice into your coffee, a small miracle happens. What's the miracle? Write a few story lines suggested by each title. But don't write what we already know. Use your imagination. There is no wrong answer there.

Go on a title expedition. Visit a store where you don't ever shop. See how creative you can be with merchandise as titles. Maybe "Brooks Brothers" is a song about a girl in love with twins and can't decide which brother she wants to see tonight. Another title could be "7-11." We have to sneak away to be together. I wish I could wake up with you next to me, but it's only safe from seven to eleven.

Sometimes, great titles come from putting words next to each other that normally don't go together. That's called juxtaposition. Like Happy Beheading. Whatever names you see, ask yourself, what else could that be?

NO COPYRIGHT FOR TITLES

You can't protect a title with a copyright. But don't recycle someone else's song name, even if the original was released decades ago. Should I discover a title has been used before, I either change it completely or add some words in parentheses to differentiate it from preexisting hits with the same name.

Even though you can't copyright titles, it would be self-destructive to attempt to write a new tune with a classic name. Like "The Long and Winding Road." Or "Born in the USA." Or "One Margarita." Or "drivers license." Even if a publisher is willing to go with a recycled title and pitches it to an artist or producer, the chances are good they'll know their hit history and turn your version down. And even if someone does record it, expect it to be a nightmare tracking your royalties.

KEEP IT SHORT

When I began my career as a staffwriter at Almo Music in Hollywood, my titles were so long they wouldn't fit on record labels. Now I know they should be short and punchy. Remember my tune "In My Dreams I was Never in Omaha," which I wrote with Steve Dorff? Neither does anyone else. How about "Take Your Suitcase out of My Life," which I played and sang in a key nobody'd ever heard before, accompanied by my baritone ukulele, to audition for the Songwriters Workshop at Capitol Records? That one got the loudest NO! in the history of music. If I were writing that first song now, I'd simply call it "Omaha." And the second would be "Suitcase."

PICTURE TITLES

For five years, I worked 24/8 to get the attention of Cher's producer. A Texas-grown eccentric from the Hollywood home for the short, he danced on his desk and fired his "pistoles" into the ceiling tiles when he heard a strong, visual title. From that I learned that when a real song person hears a sizzle song name, all hell breaks loose. Doors that were welded shut burst open. Powerful people who can say yes take you to lunch at restaurants where there aren't any prices on the menu. They send you cases of wine that you can trade for a Tesla on miscellaneous Wednesdays. Your lawyer takes your calls, and journalists finally spell your surname correctly.

I forced myself to learn to write visually when Cher was cutting all those big-hooked songs like "Gypsys, Tramps & Thieves," "Dark Lady," and "Half-Breed." I didn't just *want* her to cut my songs, I *needed* her to. Eventually she did, but she went into labor that night at the studio and Elijah Blue Allman popped out before his momma got to do the second verse. So there went that.

However, I continued writing story songs. A Canadian, I also taught myself the geography of the southern states to make my tales ring true. That took watching a lot of episodes of *Jeopardy!* To this day, unless specifically instructed not to, I love writing visually. If you can hear a song, that's one sense. If you can see it, that's two. The more senses your songs appeal to, the bigger the impact.

Story-structure training helped me write and sell five screen-plays in two years, bought me my first home, and showed me how I could quickly help my songwriting clients with their story problems.

Great titles open big doors. Just remember, once you get in, make sure your whole song is as powerful, passionate, and orig-inal as your title.

You can do this. Honest.

CHAPTER 5

CO-WRITING

When you co-write, I suggest you always do what's best for your song, not your ego. Stick that on the side of your monitor. Always do what's best for your song.

A song should sound like a seamless work, whether it's written by one person or five. It should *not* sound like one person's words set to someone else's music or track. It is one expression.

If someone writes the melody first, and it inspires you to write the words, stick as closely as you can to that tune. It's the part that draws in your audience first. Later, you and the composer can negotiate changing this and that note.

If you write the words first, give your melody writer the freedom to take words and/or syllables out. Most important is making your song sing. It's not a poem set to music.

Be very gentle with suggestions to your co-writer. He/she is as sensitive as you are, if not more so. If there's something you don't like, try this: "Line four is nice. What else could it be?" That way, nobody is being trampled.

You want to feel like a team. Not I did this and you did that; and my part's fine but man, right here? Yuck. Imagine the roles were reversed. "Molly, this part feels haphazard" is not revision-endearing. How about, "Could we look at line two together?"

The wordsmith's job is to translate the feelings of the music and rhythm into words. The words have to "sing." They should flow easily and comfortably with the melody.

The words don't have to be 1,000 percent true. I suggest my clients start with the truth and make it more interesting in their lyrics. Same with their melodies. There is never only one tune for each line, and there could be dozens of different rhythms to try.

A good contemporary lyric is often the equivalent of dialogue. So I suggest you eavesdrop. Write down what you overhear people saying, especially teens. The rhythms are there too. Chances are good you'll be able to use some lines and rhythms of their conversations for your lyrics and music.

PUT THE STRESSES IN THE RIGHT PLACES

Be careful not to em**pha**size the wrong syl**lab**le in order to accommodate the music. If you find you're doing that, tweak the lyric so the stresses are natural. A trick I use instead of mis-stressing "fanta-**sea**," a body of water in which a bad lyric may drown, is to add an extra syllable to "sea-ee." Hopefully, your co-writer will let you have that extra syllable or note. Again, remember, always do what's best for your song.

Since the melody and rhythm rule the song (lyricists, sorry, yes, it's true), I usually don't ask my co-writers to revise the tune too much, and neither should you. The last thing you want to do is mess with the magic of that melody, especially the hooks.

Music can have any meter. So if you write lyrics with long lines of iambic pentameter, I suggest you give your co-writer the freedom to take words and phrases out here and there to make the melody, and its rhythm, unpredictable. As songwriters, we're in the business of surprises.

If you have a $1,000,000 title, your collaborator should first try to accommodate it. That could simply mean placing it somewhere you didn't expect it to be. The bottom line in any successful collaboration is flexibility. Do what's best for the song. Always do what's best for the song.

Knowing who my song is for helps me create it. Then I have focus. It's not just another song tossed out there on the web, aching for acceptance. Ostensibly, it already has a home.

You're not married to a lyric or a melody, no matter how long you've walked around with that phrase in your head or in a digital file before meeting up with your partner. Again, accommodate one another. Always do what's best for your song, not your ego.

Since nobody hums a lyric, wordsmiths have to bow to the melody and rhythm. Those latter two components draw in the audience. If, and only if, they prevail, after hearing and feeling the tune three or four times, *then* the audience is aware of the words. So let the melody and rhythm do their jobs first, then the words kick in to cinch the deal.

I know that's a devastating blow to you lyricists. It's like being whacked repeatedly on the side of your head. But it's the truth. Researchers have actually hooked humans up to machines and tested random audience responses. They found that rhythm and melody draw people in initially. The words keep them there. Without lyricists, there would be nothing to sing. All vocalists would be instantly replaced by trombones.

BE PROUD

I want you to be proud of being a wordsmith. Please, never say, "I only write lyrics." Instead, stand up tall and straight, yelling into a mirror, at the top of your voice, "**I WRITE LYRICS**!" Do that several times a day.

I used to be intimidated by the glorious, soaring music themes created for movies and TV by my collaborators. But not anymore. I'm proud of the melodies I create, on my own, from scratch. But I remember the days when I was introduced as "This is my lyricist," or "Toodles's writing partner." Jeeze.

No matter who your co-writer is, like everything else in the music business, before you begin, sign an agreement saying something like this: if the song we attempt to write together doesn't work out, I am entitled to take back the part I contributed, as are you, with yours. Y'never know.

If you write alone, you're still co-writing—with your critic—who never likes anything. Ever. But make it one of your missions to ignore that smarmy, snaggy voice, whose job is to keep you miserable. To squash him, and shut him up, imagine you're wearing headphones. The one covering your left ear broadcasts your sweet, spontaneous, creative voice. Crank up that volume, and pull the plug completely on the other guy.

CONTEMPORARY CO-WRITING

If you're invited to co-write in a contemporary situation, some-times with up to ten people, it's usually a positive, spontaneous experience. There's usually an artist who is part of the team, waiting for your song. You're "in the room" with talented writers, producers, and avalanches of ideas, riffs, and rhythm. Somebody hums something, someone else throws out a title, the guy in that cute blue shirt suggests a line. One idea inspires another. This project usually has a tight deadline. You're not just writing a song, it's a whole track too. And it has a home, going in.

When it's finished, even though it's impossible to deter-mine who did what, everyone in the room, including the kid who delivers the croissants, is your co-writer. Even if you wrote the whole melody, 10 percent of a hit is better than 100 percent of "maybe some other time."

The key here is to be invited into the room. Here's where networking takes over as your best talent. For example, if you wrote with Suzanne, who co-wrote with Angelina, who played bass on the second single with George and Jack, who is in Johnny's band. That's how the music collaboration business works today. Not only do you have to be original, have a resume, but you need to be a good networker too. It's like social climbing, which I call collab-climbing.

Stay on it. You can do this. I promise. Just go after it, a few hours a day, every day. Then practice your acceptance speech as you prepare to revel as your name is called with the artist's whole posse at the Grammys. Ask any songwriter. We all have our speeches ready, because y'never know.

TESTING THE MELODY

If you create the words to a melody that's already written, the trick to seeing if the song is as strong as it needs to be in order to realistically compete in a highly competitive marketplace is this: Would those words have inspired that melody? If the melody came first, would those notes have inspired your words?

Those are tough questions, but truthful answers save you a lot of grief down the road when somebody says I love the words but not the tune. Or vice versa. Then what?

Be diplomatic. If you say, I hate that, or that's not any good, you'll shut down your partner. Instead, I suggest you fudge a little, and say, "hey, that's good, what else y'got hiding in your guitar today?"

A major stumbling block for collaborators is possessiveness. Sometimes teams work exclusively with one another. They make commitments just as they do in any other business deal. But some co-writing situations are more casual, with both partners working with other people. My advice is not to focus on what you DON'T do together, but on what you DO accomplish as a team.

If your partner is suddenly successful with another tune-smith, it's natural for you to be jealous. But remember, your co-writer is also the co-author of the songs you wrote together. His/her success is contagious. Step up and be the first one to cheer his/her victory, be gracious about it, and use that hit to haul out the ones created with you.

Nobody can explain why one co-writing team works and another fizzles. Try to give each new association a fair shot. It doesn't always take in the first song, so go with it for a couple more. By then, you'll know if it's magic or mediocre. If an old partner of yours is suddenly successful with someone else, figure your turn with your current co-writer is coming up too, and keep working.

Even though we have so many good co-writing apps now, allowing us to partner with someone in Botswana or Berlin, sometimes collaborations are a matter of convenience. You may be the only two musical people in your zip code. At first, you were both in the same place in terms of your careers. You had everything ahead of you and nothing but enthusiasm for your team effort. But suppose you feel that your partner isn't holding up his or her end of the bargain. Maybe your co-writer is not as committed as you are to becoming a hit songwriter anymore. Perhaps they are cranking out the same melody, sideways, every time you get together. Or maybe you've just outgrown each other. Could be your melodies have been steadily improving but their lyrics aren't. *That's* a dilemma.

Suppose you pushed and encouraged your partner to dig deeper and come up with something more original, but nothing changes. This is the time when you might suggest bringing in a third writer. The chemistry will certainly change, and y'never know. And if that flops, you have to make one of the toughest decisions of your life.

Here's where you both try working with other people. For a while. Don't sever the relationship permanently because your present partner could just be going through a slump. Something could happen in six days or six months to trigger a spark of greatness. You owe it to your songs to make them as good as they have to be in order to realistically compete. Tell your co-writer that you want to work with some different tunesmiths to try stretching new muscles in your brain. Put the onus on yourself, not your partner. Truthfully, your heart knows when your collaboration is sizzling. When it isn't, you have the choice of either being a victim to it or taking charge. The people with hit songs take charge.

This breaking up process is exactly like ending a marriage. It's emotionally grinding, devastating, debilitating, and terrifying; but, in the end, for the best. It's especially excruciating if you write with your spouse, a roommate, or a relative. If you think working with different partners will damage your personal relationship and if you feel that's more important than your songwriting career—fine. Stay where you are. But if your career is more important, you have to muster the courage to be honest. If your current partner is really cheering for you, they will understand eventually and become your biggest fan.

Writing is a risk. So is moving on. But without taking chances, as artists, our hearts will shut down and die. We'd be comatose, living boring, safe, predictable lives, because as creators, we're missing the top layer of skin, so our nerve endings are always raw. Our songs can't be boring, safe, or predictable. They have to soar, sail, be inventive, exciting, original, and right on the edge of the edge. Having a creative spirit means ignoring the easy doors marked yes and plowing right through the ones that say no, anyway, to see what is waiting for us on the other side. We take chances every minute of every day in our lives. That's who we are. Period. And that's who our writing partners are too.

When I write without a melody as a guide, I have too much freedom. I may write something that is articulate but dull from a rhythmic point of view. I tend to use too many syllables. Although I know better, sometimes there's a part of me that aches to paint a more vivid picture in the lyric or describe an emotion in greater detail. Then I end up with long lines of fifteen or sixteen syllables each and wonder why my co-writer can't come up with a melody that rocks.

So for me, being in the room with my partner and creating simultaneously works best. This way, I don't go off on any tangents and my partner doesn't have to go through my lyric with a nasty red pencil, scratching out all my heart-sought adjectives.

This process works best when I'm working with someone I trust. That means I can suggest a terrible line or phrase and not worry that my partner is going to groan and moan and think I can't do any better. I may come up with forty stupid ideas, but my partner knows from past experience that idea forty-one could be the gem we've been waiting for all day.

Trust is the major ingredient in any successful partnership, because you give each other permission to risk being bad. With trust, you know how to deal with the near misses. And you've learned from your past experiences together how to urge your partner on in a new direction when they have been stumbling with the same stuck melody or set of words all day. I feel that without trust, you are auditioning, not writing.

Every co-write is different. I always suggest you create from strength, not fear. This is just as true when you write by yourself. Whichever method of collaboration works best for you, it's vital to understand the subtleties of the relationship with your partner. If something isn't working, you can stand back and be objective. In a successful collaboration, ideally, no one should dominate or control the situation. Your job is to hook up with your partner's magic and vice versa.

I BLEW IT

On the first few occasions in my career when my agent arranged for me to co-write with a "star," I was so intimidated by the guy's resume, and I wrote badly. I'm talkin' embarrassingly trite. It didn't occur to me that the "star" knew my work, was familiar with what I could do, or he wouldn't have set aside time to work with me in the first place. Back then, all I could tell myself was "I blew it." As a result, I slouched home, climbed under my duvet, and sulked there for six weeks.

Now I feel confident to the point of being cocky, and know that when the wind and stars are aligned, and the chemistry is just so, I can write like the best of 'em. I'm pumped up and ready for anything. Bring it. My wish for you is to share that confidence as you enter each new co-writing session.

While writing, if it feels right to compose a ballad, fine. However, now rhythm rules. Since almost every successful tune-smith has access to software called Pro Tools, we can make very slick, sophisticated recordings at home for very little money. Record companies, music publishers, music supervisors, and all other outlets expect and only consider finished masters. So the ears of the music industry have become much more demanding in terms of the quality of our productions.

Because of this, songwriters who aren't producers face a quandary. Should they include the recording engineer as a co-writer?

Here's what I do. I simply ask the engineer straight out what he wants. If he decides he prefers a handsome payment for the track, that's it. Or perhaps that sum plus some of the publishing? Or, I let him spell it all out, we sign an agreement that makes us both happy, and away we go.

But nobody does anything without that signed agreement. EVER.

Even if a producer opts for just the money, when my songs are licensed and recorded, I send him a percentage of my earnings anyway. I mean, hey, I'm not going to miss 10 percent of what could be millions of dollars, and my producer feels proud and credited for his good work.

It's no secret I have the tech chops of a nice green plant. So I laugh at myself when I'm writing a new song and have to record myself singing it a cappella. A Molly demo is really a treat, especially for the deaf. Nonetheless, once I know the singer's key, I send that information with my digital recording to our engineer. In my head, I know how I want the production to sound. But how I *hear* it and how I can *play* it are two different things. That's where a good arranger comes in. Thank God.

Like me, all creative people are very sensitive. We have fragile egos. I have to be careful about what I say to keep everybody feeling good and important so that they can produce their best work. I only hire professional people who do excellent work and give me and my clients their best. But occasionally I run into some brick walls that no one in any other business would ever believe.

I'm not a member of the United States Senate. I don't sell cryptocurrency and have no inclination to perform root canals for fun or profit on long weekends in July. I am a songwriter. I live and breathe my craft, and I'm committed to doing my best work every time out.

I actually love it when my engineer/arranger says, "Molly, line three? C'mon, girl. You can do better." My clients and my songs deserve my very best every time out. So I only work with people who bring that same integrity and energy to the table.

NEVER AGAIN

Several years ago, I found a singer who had a once-in-a-lifetime voice and sang my feelings more deeply than I felt them. So I hired her to do all my recordings.

Let's call her Puffy. She and her husband, Pete, had a recording studio in their home. He cut my tracks and she did the vocals. We were cookin'. My songs were getting cut, it was good publicity for the studio and Puffy's vocal career.

But then a monumental breach of ethics occurred. My co-writer was flying from New York to LA, specifically to be at our 11 a.m. session. I confirmed several times with P&P, reminding them to be careful not to schedule any sessions too close to ours in case we ran late. Nonetheless, the day of the session, as my hopeful co-writer landed at LAX, Pete called, saying Puffy had taken a better paying gig before ours, and wouldn't be able to sing for us after all. *What?*

My co-writer had already flown across the country, landed at LAX, I'd been on Highway 101 heading south to the studio for an hour when I got this news. Trying to stay calm, I pulled over to the side of the road for half an hour, just breathing. But I was seething with rage. In the end, Puffy showed up a few days later, sang our song but without any passion. She was just singing words. I had to do it all over again at another studio, with a different singer.

By the way, P&P insisted on keeping the money I paid them up front. *Really?*

It was important for me to tell them how upset I was that they disregarded and disrespected the value of my co-writer's time and our money. But as long as I've been in the music business, dealing with dysfunctional maniacs, I've never had a phone message like the one Pete left, saying they really wished I would bring more professional people to their studio who could understand when something more important came up.

Really? I thought he might have called to apologize. But not Pete. What's more important than a commitment? So *their* breach was *my* fault?

To this day, I'm still shocked that Puffy and Pete would dismiss my co-writer's feelings, and mine, with the twisted thinking that it was *our* problem for being unprofessional.

Jesus.

That was the end of that team. Puffy is still Puffy. She's still singing oohs instead of being a solo artist on a real label. I guess that's as much success as she can handle.

Stories like this one show how it doesn't take long to discover why very talented people never achieve the success they deserve. The sad part is they're never responsible for anything. It's never their fault.

When this happened, it felt like a death to me. I'd lost the production arm of my company. But after a lot of long, uphill walks across the sunrise, I realized the world is full of great singers and engineers. Eventually, I simply found a new team.

Some collaborations last forever. For others, it's the weekend. Some don't even make it as far as the chorus. But that's how it is with creative, sensitive people. It's devastating—absolutely devastating—every time a team of any kind splits apart. But you move on, releasing your sadness like bad breadcrumbs along the way to the next new project down the road.

When you strike gold collaborating with someone new, you realize you never would have written those tunes if you hadn't been dumped. And you celebrate trusting the universe to get you the rest of the way, down a hidden path ahead.

Your job is to show up.

FOCUS ON SONGWRITING

INSIDER ADVICE FROM CARL STURKEN AND EVAN ROGERS, WRITERS/PRODUCERS/PUBLISHERS, RIHANNA

When I need to talk to somebody, but don't have a direct connection, I stay on it until I find a way to hook up. Some people say that's pushy. These days, it sounds better describing it as networking.

When I signed the contract to write this book, my agent, Roger Williams, told me he was glad I had so many funny stories to share. For years, he had been encouraging his friend, mega writer/producer Carl Sturken, to write his own book, but Carl wasn't interested. Nonetheless, Roger kindly arranged an introduction with half of one of the most successful writer/producer teams in the history of our business.

Carl Sturken studied music at Wesleyan. He didn't like the way it was taught, so he took private lessons from Tony Purrone, who had played with Miles Davis.

"The man could play anything a human could play," Carl told me. Then he became the guitarist in a funk band called Too Much Too Soon. He and his partner, Evan Rogers, wanted to be the next Earth, Wind & Fire. "We were great musicians," Carl said. "But it wasn't happening."

However, they kept writing songs. "Evan had a great voice. He took the bus down from Connecticut, slept on my couch, and we wrote all day, every day."

They worked with Black bands in Black venues. "We were the white guys."

"Out of nowhere, the owner of the club, Leviticus, asked me if I wanted to produce records for him." What? Carl had no clue what that meant, but he said yes.

Meanwhile, Evan made a record that sold four copies. And when he and Carl did an album called *Hold On*, they couldn't get any radio station to play it. "This is an example of how getting a record deal doesn't mean a clear shot to stardom. You got yourself on the football team, you're in a uniform, but you haven't scored a touchdown yet, so it's not time to celebrate."

As for songwriting, Carl never had a lesson other than trying and failing. Being around other writers was the key. "I learned from imitating hit records."

Rogers/Sturken's first gig as writer/producers was "Heartbreaker" for Evelyn "Champagne" King. The single was recorded on an 8-track. In those days, production budgets were all-in. "We kept what was left after the track was complete. Labels were paying seventy-five hundred dollars per cut.

"We had two tracks on Britney Spears's first CD on Jive Records when she was fifteen, but when we signed with Universal, instead of Jive, those tracks mysteriously disappeared from her project.

"Then, in 1986, we were paid one hundred thousand dollars to record ten tracks for Tasha Holiday. In the late nineties, while star writers and producers Jimmy Jam and Terry

Lewis were paid fifty thousand dollars per track, by 2010, when the industry was in crisis, that fee plummeted for us to twelve thousand and five hundred dollars. Sales were way, way down and record companies were merging. Between 2010 and 2015, Evan and I thought it was the end.

"Everyone was afraid streaming would devastate the business. Now, it represents 50 percent of record companies' revenue.

"You need to spend your time writing a better song," Carl said. "You need to be an expert on writing hit songs. Don't go to engineering school. Use Garage Band on your phone. Focus on songwriting.

"Our lives changed when Evan, our wives, and I were in Barbados for Christmas. We were introduced to a beautiful, young girl singer there. She was a little pitchy but sang promising R&B and catchy pop. Her name was Rihanna.

"We worked with her for two years, grooming her sound and presence. When 'Pon de Replay' crossed our desk, it sounded like a nursery rhyme with a great hook. Alisha Brooks and Vada Nobles wrote a great tune, which we tweaked and immediately called Rihanna to come up to New York to sing for us.

"But Def Jam, her label, wasn't happy with the record. Her career could've been over. However, we got it to radio station Z100 ourselves, in New York City. They loved it. Pop fans heard it and loved it too. I lost my mind!

"We were two white guys working in R&B, and didn't make pop records for eight years. For those Rihanna records, we were writers and producers. Ninety-five percent of our income for her projects came from song-writing/publishing income.

"Not long after the Rihanna sensation, Gemma Corfield at Virgin records called us up. We'd been making R&B records. Could we do Donny Osmond? Sure. Donny was the whitest guy. If we could have a hit with him, we're not just R&B, we're pop too.

"For that project, we worked fast, even with background singers and lots of musicians. We produced five-hundred-dollar demos in three to four hours. And we learned to make our tracks sound like masters.

"At the time, we were paid fifteen thousand dollars per track. Expenses were seven thousand dollars. We kept the rest, plus three or four points. We were writers *and* producers, so we did well. Like in the movies, record company accounting is so squirrely, you rarely make money just as a producer—it's all a loss on paper.

"We were in the first wave of writer/ producers. I focused on making demos that sounded like masters. Evan is a great singer, so we got a great sound, plus lots of gigs.

"One thing that worked for us was producing recordings that sounded great with just one instrument and one voice. It works for some songs if they're great songs. We were clear about writing songs with production and songs that work for just one voice, one instrument.

"If you have a specific sound, it may go stale, so you have to keep reinventing yourself.

"A pure song is one you could sit down and play in any version and everyone would get it.

"One of our strengths in lasting so long is understanding how to proceed as songwriters and producers. When we signed with MCA, we were making R&B records. But Leeds Levy, the president, was straight with us:

'You're good, but if you want to go to the next level, you need to work on your lyrics.'

"At first, we were mad, but he was right. Leeds set us up with his MCA writers Brock Walsh, Robbie Neville, Mark Muller, Glen Ballard, and Siedah Garrett. They pored over our lyrics, plotting the stories. We'd never thought of doing that. Evan and I observed how our fellow staff writers created the words, and we adapted their techniques. MCA put us with a different writer every day. I remember when Leeds saw one of our titles and said, 'I think we can do better than that.' Evan and I were startled that he was so brutal, but he was right. Leeds Levy was a strong song man, and MCA was a great training ground for us.

"There's heavy politics involved in the business of music. Evan and I have made a lot of records and let the artists contribute as writers, even if we wrote the songs ourselves. Half of fifty million dollars is better than 100 percent of nothin'.

"When we met with an artist, we'd do four sides. Although the singers were often not very good writers, we'd fool them into thinking they were. We'd make it look like we were stuck (on a song we'd already written) and they saved the day with an obvious line. We were great actors.

"If it'll improve the song and its chances of success, we always bring in another person. In a world where you write a word and take a third, you have to roll with it. Even more than our talent, Evan and I try hard to make smart decisions. We're not geniuses, but we've become smart. That's how you survive.

"One of the most important things for someone trying to make their way is this: when your inspiration is love of music, but you're hoping to make a living from it, those two things don't necessarily work together. What's most important is to be very, very clear on what you're trying to do. When I produced my first record, my goal was to make as much money as possible with anyone who will take my songs. I never confused that with artistry.

"Throughout our career, Evan and I have been like heat-seeking missiles. We wanted to do whatever was hot. So, if you're following your artistic vision, fine, but you can't serve two masters at the same time. Pick one."

EVAN ROGERS

Evan Rogers is the singer in the Sturken/Rogers success team. He and Carl are best friends, co-writers, and co-producers. Evan told me, "We have a chemistry in business, as partners and song-writers. Carl and I share the same values in treating people. We do it right. We treat people as we would want to be treated."

Evan knows the way the current marketplace is evolving.

"I tend to be much more involved with our company's marketing and business. As of this writing, the perfect model for launching new artists is Billie Eilish. What she does applies to all new acts launching now.

"Before she entered the public conscious-ness, breaking in as a new artist was about a bunch of label people deciding his/her fate, the track, and the radio push.

"But it all changed with Billie. First, she put her music on SoundCloud. It's a place where kids can discover music for free. She added Spotify, where the same kids also hang out, but have to pay to listen. Billie struck a nerve with really honest music, which was a complete open book of her raw, teenage feelings. She didn't have a genre. She was making music that didn't fit in any radio format. Yet, it was so honest. Her songs connected with the kids.

"She approached her career without any thought of a label or radio. She just kept putting out music with cool videos, and built a following that swelled and roared in like a tsunami.

"Billie Eilish became a star by letting the fans decide. She put out songs, not pre-packed singles. Songs. One at a time. She did this for two years without going to radio and yet, she sold out arenas.

"Finally, radio came to the party. They played music never heard on pop stations. Station managers realized they had to include songs they normally wouldn't, so they could give the kids what they wanted.

"Now, as new young fans discover Eilish, they grow with her as a family, a team. She and Finneas, her genius writer/producer brother, are writing honest, devastating songs on the laptop in his bedroom. As they create a new track, they don't ask if radio programmers will like it. They write from Billie's tortured soul, and the kids who share that scorching pain fall in love with her.

"She'd never had a big hit single, but Eilish sure had a following. The influencers on TikTok were all about her." They're twelve-year-olds, who went directly from hopscotch to hype, and are paid $200,000+ a year by record labels, as promoters. And ultimately, Interscope signed her.

"Radio is still important, but more and more, kids are streaming—YouTube, Spotify, and Apple Music. To them, radio is for old people.

"The biggest thing now is TikTok. People put up little short clips of dancing, balancing on their heads, or wearing chainsaws in a chartreuse, polka dot bubble bath. The clips are eight to fifteen seconds long. Then, other people put music behind them, so there's always a song in the background. If the video blows up on TikTok, you're set. That platform doesn't pay royalties, but it has become the ultimate launching pad. Record companies are now paying these twelve-year-old influencers whatever they want to use their artist's song in those TikTok videos.

"With hits, you go on tour, play the arenas, and eventually, it's standing-room only. Then the major labels chase you to sign with them. But before that happens, without even listening to your music, some business affairs guy needs to know how many social media followers you have. Labels want you to do their initial promotional work for them.

"Neither Carl nor I ever had a plan B. Maybe that's how to stay in it. I never really had a job. And if I'd been born rich, I'd still be doing this.

"These days, a great way to launch a song-writing career is to co-write with someone who's just a step ahead of you. Then, ideally, you're invited to be "in the room" to bring your finger-print to share with other writers, producers, and artists while new songs and tracks are created. Then, your name is on current work, and who knows, maybe a hit. You're building momentum and creating a resume. Even if you only receive a fraction of what you'd get for writing a whole song by yourself, the trade-off is you're part of the team."

CHAPTER 6

MAKING TIME TO WRITE

I'm old school. I still use a ring-bound, Sierra Club planner/appointment book, along with an actual pen, to write down my daily commitments. In the top left corner of each day's "slot," I write a W. That letter stands for Write. Sometimes I use WW, which means Write Well. Sorry, Oprah.

Looking at my calendar every night before I go to sleep, and again first thing each morning, I see my promise to spend time creating at a specific hour. I'm a morning person, so it's usually 5:00 a.m. I wake up early because that's when my fiber-deficient neighbor starts clanging his pots and pans. He follows that with leaf blowing, and I'm tired of hurling tomatoes at him over the fence. Getting an early start also helps me accommodate my co-writers and consulting clients in different time zones.

So—5:00 a.m. There's me, shuffling to my desk or my keyboard or both. It's my job to write every day, especially when I have a large project, like this book. I know I'm not going to finish the whole thing in a week. Or a year. But if I do a little bit every day, eventually there it is, all finished, at Barnes & Noble.

Novelist Irving Wallace told me he never sat down to write a novel. Instead, his goal was to create only one good page a day. And, 365 days later, he had a whole book. If he can do it, we should all try his process.

I am a disciplined wordsmith. No matter what else is happening in the world, my job is to create something new every morning. When I'm finished that day's work, I check it off in my appointment book, telling myself, "Good for me." I also agree not to determine whether what I have on the page is good, bad, or promising until tomorrow. Then, I come back to my notes from the previous day and see what flies. The main thing here is that I showed up, my computer as well as my pen were busy, and the check mark in my calendar proves I completed my daily assignment. That's momentum.

When I look back at my calendar for the whole week, there are lots of check marks, proving I did my pages. I did it. I did it. I didn't cheat and SAY I showed up. I was really there. Keeping that commitment every day makes me feel accomplished. Now, the stack of paper in the brown FedEx box is getting thicker. Looks good. Feels good too.

Time and distance will tell me whether what I wrote is worth keeping, tweaking, or setting aside for now. Maybe I just save a word or a few notes. Nonetheless, there is something new every day.

I'm lucky in that I work from home. I've always set my own schedule. I can do what I want when I want, and there's nobody noodging me, "Come on, Molly, come on, Molly, come on, Molly, get to work, get to work, get to work. Stop schlocking around and start writing."

Even though I don't have a boss, my critic is on duty 24/8 (not a typo), so there really is somebody here, with a deep, booming voice, waking me up, hollering, "Get outta bed. Eat your breakfast, do your yoga, brew your chamomile tea, start writing…"

But there are days I just don't feel like it. For example, this morning there are two garage sales I want to visit, but I can't leave until I finish my pages.

Here was my discussion with me this morning.

Hey—look at all the work I've already done. Good, eh? Would it be okay if I just ran up the hill to the garage sale for twenty minutes and THEN got to work? I mean it's just a few blocks away and...

No. Get your writing done first. Then go.

But if I don't get there early, all the good stuff will be gone.

You took several hours off yesterday to donate blood and get your teeth cleaned. I'd like you to write a few hours this morning.

But...

No "buts." If you break your commitment today, you could get in the habit of letting it slide. You know you'll lose your rhythm, and your book isn't going to write itself.

Could I have breakfast first?

Yes. But save the crossword puzzle until after you've got a few new pages.

Okay, I can do that. But are you sure I can't go to that garage sale?

All creative people have those conversations with themselves every morning.

I usually work on assignment and have tight deadlines. If I blow it, there go my connections who have been licensing my original work in movies, TV shows, video games, and commercials for a long, lovely time. Don't even ask how many years it took me to build that network. Do I really want to blow it all on the fifty-nine-cent teacup I could find at a garage sale, then trash it, because it has a chip?

Whenever you're torn, keep thinking of your song as a gift from the universe that you were chosen to write. Aside from the exhilarating rush of creating something original, your new tune could support you nicely down the road. But first you have to finish it. So, give it your focus every day, even if only for a few minutes. Think of it as a child, needing your attention. You wouldn't turn away from his adorable, chocolate-covered smile, would you?

THE CRITIC

We're all plagued with voices telling us we're not writing, even when we are. That's our critic. No matter how well we're doing, he attempts to shut us down by yelling we could be doing more and doing better. All these years later, I still hear, "I sent you to college. When are you going to get a real job?"

See what I mean?

AFFIRMATIONS

When I finish a writing session I tell myself, out loud, that I did a good job, that I came up with a few good lines or a good start, and I should be very proud of myself. This affirmation, along with others I'll list later, helps to drown out the critic who will never give any of us credit for doing anything right. Even on the Grammy stage, while everybody is cheering for our win, he'll tell us we blew it because the shoes we chose are dead wrong.

Here are some of the affirmations I say out loud each morning:

> I am a creative spirit with amazing gifts to share with the world.

> I am unique.

> I write my fingerprint.

> I'm proud of who I am and what I do.

> Even if my page is blank, my subconscious is working 24/7.

> I can do this.

> I am on the edge of miracles in my song-writing career every day.

> It only takes one yes to get to everything I want.

> I believe in me even when nobody else does.

> I have something to contribute to the literature of music that nobody else can, because nobody but me, is me.

> Good for me!

KILL YOUR CRITIC

Remember the headphones example from earlier in the book? It's important so I'm going to repeat it. Let's say we're always wearing headphones on both ears. In our happy one, there's an inspired, positive, nurturing voice telling us what we're doing and what we've done is excellent, promising, working well, and good for us. The jerk in the other ear has only one smarmy mission: to squash us with golf shoes and glee. But we can quickly shut up this dude by simply unplugging his side of our headphones.

Done.

The trick is to continually remind ourselves to pull that plug.

FIND YOUR PRIVATE CREATIVE SPACE

I suggest you create a place for you to write where you can shut out distractions. One of my clients works in a corner of his basement. Another is most productive in the back seat of his car in the garage. Another sits on the floor of her closet with her laptop and keyboard.

All of these spaces are sacred. Nothing—absolutely nothing—and no one is allowed to interrupt these writers there while they're working. Period.

There's a wonderful movie called *My Salinger Year*. In it, J.D. says to make fifteen minutes for your writing every day in a space that's sacred. Nobody can interrupt you then and there. I agree. You'll be amazed how productive you can be in that short a time. I say to myself, "Well, I'll give it a shot. I'll see what I can do before my yoga class. I mean I'm not expecting the next 'One Margarita' to come dancing out of me in just that short time." And y'know, without any demand, I always surprise myself by what I start during that "give it a shot" few minutes.

No matter how successful we become as songwriters, it's still better to wish we had more time to write then ache for more to write about.

As I said earlier, one art inspires another.

I'm as passionate about visual art as I am about songwriting. Visiting museums and galleries is as vital to me as breathing. What I discover on those walls is always inspiring. For example, after watching David Hockney's "Seven Yorkshire Landscape Videos" at the Los Angeles County Museum of Art from the second row, I was dazzled and wanted to view it again. But the usher made me leave the screening theatre to make room for a new group. However, I found an empty seat in a different section of the theatre and sneaked back in.

From that new point of view, I saw a completely different film. Hockney deliberately placed his cameras so that would happen. Stunned, I drove straight home and wrote a song called "The Road That Wasn't There." I even sent it to Hockney, although I had no idea if he ever received my mp3. A few years later, when I met him in LA at an opening, he sang my chorus back to me.

A lot of my colleagues are wonderful cooks. Their Facebook photos are more enticing every day. Some writers tend to extraordinary gardens. Others keep painting and repainting the same wall with different colors and designs. It's all the same creative energy, swirling around us. Our job is to reach up and pick a miracle to write about today.

KNOW WHEN NOT TO WRITE

As important as it is to make time to write, it's equally essential for any successful writer and artist to know when he or she needs a day off.

For ten years of weekday mornings at Marjan's Deli in the Brentwood Country Mart in Los Angeles, I had breakfast with Carol Sobieski. She was THE sought-after screenwriter, one of the busiest in the world. Carol was always writing. Refusing to use computers, she even brought her yellow legal papers with scribbles on them to breakfast.

However, once every ten days or so, she took a day off, got herself a roll of quarters plus a large box of Tide, and roared off in her yellow Honda for a laundry run. Heading north up the Pacific coast from LA, she visited all three of her kids who were attending boarding schools within a couple hours' drive.

The change of agenda was very valuable to her, since she invariably came home filled with stories of her kids that exasperated her, but at the same time, went right into her Emmy-winning and Oscar-nominated scripts.

Observing her writing habits, I thought to myself, "Self, here's one of the most creative and successful women in the world. Do what she does."

A UCLA writing teacher of mine said he liked to take his notebook to museums where he would park himself on a bench and work in those crowded, cacophonous halls. For him, the more noise he had to drown out, the deeper he would have to concentrate. This man was inspired by ideas he wouldn't have gotten if he stayed home in his familiar surroundings and didn't have to concentrate so deeply.

COPING WITH ISOLATION

Like most artists, I suffer greatly from isolation. But I can spend six or eight hours alone at my piano or desk if I know I'll be seeing a live human after I finished work. Consequently, I schedule lots of dinners with friends.

YOUR SUBCONSCIOUS IS ALWAYS WORKING

After a writing session, whether it's five minutes or your lunch hour, and you reluctantly head back to your day job or home, even when you think you're just texting, folding laundry, or raking the Sycamore leaves from your patio, your subconscious never stops. It's like one of those 800 numbers in the People's Republic of Cheese, where somebody's always on duty.

While I'm watering my precious succulents or baking my famous sour cream cinnamon-raisin coffee cake, nuts optional, sure enough, an idea arrives while I'm up to my elbows in batter. My hands are all gooey and I end up fishing a perfectly good eyebrow pencil out of my purse to write on my kitchen wall. But I always write the idea down.

I believe it's on us to save everything that chooses us to write it. To me, it's like those yellow cabs we used to see in long lines at airports. If you don't choose the thought at the front of the line in the first cab, someone else grabs it and drives away. Okay, then you're waiting for a better concept when cab two is hailed by another person, and he drives off too. Then all the yellow cabs are gone. You're standing there on the curb. How long will you have to stay there until the next batch of yellow cabs and inspirations appear? Honor whatever comes into your head. Y'never know.

Whenever I get a new flash that makes me dance, I write it down. If I don't, I've learned the hard way it'll disappear into someone else's imagination. Then a week later, I could tune into my favorite station and hear the song I didn't write, singing to me.

WRITE SOMETHING SILLY

I don't always write songs. Sometimes it's a letter to myself, reminding me how well I did the day before. Often, it's a note to the gardener reminding him to prune my Jacaranda tree. I may even revise that missive nine times, but the point is, no matter what I'm putting on paper, it's all writing.

Doing a little every day is like oiling machinery to keep it functioning at a high level. I was advised to run the air conditioner in my car for a few minutes once a week, even during the winter, to make sure the system would work when I need it on hot, muggy summer days. Same with our imaginations.

Sometimes I do limericks. Since I create each morning, and stay warmed up, I can write one of those five-line poems between the bedroom and the kitchen, which is about forty-five feet. There's no demand on it to be brilliant, and when it's complete, I have tangible proof that I actually wrote something. Today, I posted one on my IT guy's website.

If it just isn't flowing on a particular day, and I'm trying to create an intense love tune based on the truth, I scribble lines of nonsense that rhyme with zickle. It's silly sounding and playful, plus it's a word I've never used in a tune. Once I've released the demand for gorgeous, gut-wrenching and Grammy-worthy vocabulary, those frivolous words feel safe to appear.

GET IT WHERE YOU CAN

For those unscheduled bursts of inspiration, I always keep something to write on next to the phone, in my pocket, my right shoe, purse, and car. While Jerry Corbetta, from Sugarloaf and The Classic Rock All-Stars, and I were stuck in Sunday Malibu traffic, we tapped out the rhythm and popped in a few short syllables for "Too Big for Small Talk." For the rhythm breaks, Corbetta honked his horn. Don't ask about the riders ahead of us who charged at Corbetta's 'Stang from their limos to pound on our windshield. Jerry and I always loved the song. The story of how it was written was even better.

> It's too big for small talk
> So don't walk away from us (honk) baby

We're too good together
To pretend we're (honk honk honk-ooh)
not.
There's too little love in the world
And we're lucky to find it
We're too big, too big—(honk honk honk)
for small talk.
© Red Amaryllis Music

Hey—Corbetta. Remember this one? Do you think you could ask God for a day off so we can go back to Malibu for that tuna salad you love? And hug each other for hours? I never got to say goodbye.

WRITE IT ALL DOWN

I suggest you keep a separate titles and possible concepts note-book. That way, when you have an assignment and you're feeling a little dry and you open your notebook, voila—you find every-thing you jotted down on more inspired days. Please do me one major favor. Promise that all your notebooks will be ring-bound so your precious pages can't tear off or fly away. See, I still don't trust phones or clouds to save anything.

CHAPTER 7

STIMULATING CREATIVITY

Some of us are lucky. We have so many sparkling, exciting, fresh ideas, we'll never run out. But from time to time, we may find we're going a little dry. If you've been crankin' out the same tune and set of words, sideways, for your last several songs, it's natural to feel nervous and frightened for your creative future. You swear you're doomed to spending the rest of your life wistfully remembering the exhilarating days of fire and thunder, when you were exploding with ideas and writing hits.

But it's far from over. You *can* do something about it and avoid playing victim to your muse. Here are some exercises I recommend when you're feeling dull, sluggish, and unable to pull in anything worth the ink from the air.

I want you to recognize that the creative process is cyclical. Although the subconscious never stops working, your conscious mind does need a day off now and then. So I use this time to gather new experiences, instead of staying home groaning and beating myself up. Get out of your house or office or wherever it is you write. Close the door to that area, figuratively and literally. Head for a place you've never been. I usually go to the same restaurant for breakfast every day and order the same thing. But when I'm stuck and feeling stale, I change my routine.

Instead of wearing my comfortable, thread-bare sweats, and meeting people I already know, I haul out the eyeliner, put on my best new clothes, and head for a place where I don't know anyone. In a foreign environment, I see new things, hear new things, and smell new things too. Instead of my perennial chamomile tea, I might order a cafe de boom boom au lait or espresso, so my taste buds are treated to a new experience as well.

Try it.

Eavesdrop. If people are discussing the stock market, pay attention. Listen, even though your songs are about love, not economics, someone could say something worth slipping into a future song. Y'never know.

Remember Blake Shelton's song "Minimum Wage"? In the chorus, he uses the phrase 401K. Before then, I'd never heard that in a song. It's what caught my ear. It was different.

I believe that for every new idea, our brains receive a little red neon sign that flashes in our grey cells. It says, "Interesting, stimulating, give me more." And the devoted librarians at the conservatories of music in our imaginations file it all away for later in the appropriate department.

YOUR DISGUISE ASSIGNMENT

When you meet new people, make up a persona who isn't a songwriter. Maybe you're a test pilot or a silver-medal ping pong player in the Pyrenees. I become an in vitro cardiologist: Molly Leikin, MD, instead of Molly Leikin, Songmd. It's playful, it's new. Why not?

Become your persona for twenty minutes. Don't worry if you blow it. This is a game. It's supposed to be fun. But whatever you do, don't sit there and pour your heart out to strangers about how stuck you are. The purpose of this exercise is to give yourself some time off from your problem, not compound it.

Go to a museum. Force yourself to look at works of art you might have avoided during earlier visits. You might not like Byzantine art but check it out anyway. When you see something different, you feel something new too.

Not long ago, I felt as creative as a soggy mop. So I went to see the French impressionist exhibit from the Hermitage and Pushkin museums in Russia. Not only was I totally delighted by the art, which is from my absolutely favorite genre, but I also stumbled onto a Lalique exhibit I didn't even know existed. (Lalique is a great rhyme word I haven't heard yet in a lyric.) When I left the museum, my mind was dancing with ideas. I raced home and worked until midnight, when my back quit.

If your brain has been running on empty, realize it needs fresh input to thrive. You never know how it will assimilate that information. Maybe you'll use it much later for a project you don't even know about yet. As a sensitive writer, you're like an insatiable vacuum cleaner. Your job is to absorb new experiences so you feel alive, enthusiastic, excited, interested, and stimulated. That's who you really are, isn't it?

Go to a store you haven't been to before. Look at merchandise you'd never consider buying. That could be a private jet (with a shower, of course), aluminum siding, or bongos. Listen to the salespeople pitch you their wares. They're often funny and don't need to know you're there with a secret motive. You may not need a new black Ferrari just now. The red one is fine for Wednesdays, but go into the showroom anyway. Act as if you're a serious buyer. See if there's a discount for cash. Or will they take a personal check? Remember, this is your persona. It's a game. You can handle it any way you want. Just go with the moment and have fun.

When I was writing a screenplay for Fox, there was a scene in which three divorcees go to a fine furrier with the intention of charging their whopping purchases to their ex's accounts. My friends, Nancy and Perri and I, had a party trying on the ermine, the chinchilla, and all those other politically incorrect hides, while taking each other's pictures. It was fun. We were giggling. It was a fantasy afternoon off.

A successful stimulant that works for me is going to a different supermarket. At my Gelson's, I know where everything is. Actually, I could probably go through the place blindfolded and still find everything I usually buy. But when I go to a different market, who knows where they hide the 337 varieties of tea? Aren't the Envy apples supposed to be near the plantains? Isn't that some kind of health law? And why are my bite-size Snickers the only candy that isn't on sale?

I might get mad and race to the exit in a hot huff, but the discomfort of being in a strange environment is actually very stimulating. I scope out grocery carts. One tired guy is a diaper specialist. Another, a Jim Beamer, with a case that's 10 percent off. He also has a small carton of low-fat cottage cheese. I love the juxtaposition. (And wouldn't that make a good title for a country song? Jim Beam and low-fat cottage cheese.) The woman with three overflowing shopping carts and six adorable, dancing replicas of herself is leading her family in song to "Green Eyed Lady" on her classic rock station in the canned peach department. And if I'm lyin', I'm dyin', and I ain't dead, our former congressperson is arguing with the sweet, exasperated cashier about expired Coca-Cola coupons.

I cook for myself, but darned if I'm going to buy one small baked potato plus a chicken breast, and have everyone in line whispering, "See that lady over there with the beautiful red hair? She eats alone...." So I buy all twenty-three varieties of Campbell's soup, plus some designer baby food, which I drop off on my single mom neighbor's step.

I was so inspired from typing the last three paragraphs, I had to take a whole day off from writing this chapter to jot down the gush of new song ideas comin' at me.

Try it. Not the typing, the doing. If I was distracted, amused, and entertained, you will be too.

Quick suggestions for immediate relief:

Wear two different socks.

Only put on one sock.

Wear two different shoes.

Drive a completely different route to work.

Eat chocolate cake for breakfast, lunch, and dinner.

Read a newspaper in a language you don't know.

Put your watch on the other wrist.

Walk backwards.

Listen to the top ten in Dar es Salaam.

Brush your teeth with the toothbrush in your other hand.

Gets your grey cells dancing, right?

Keep all these suggestions handy. Y'never know when you'll need them.

YELLOW PAGES

Something I do when I'm feeling a little blah is flip open the yellow pages. Yes, that book is still delivered, although in my house, its use is for propping up chairs for little blonde toddlers who call me Maw-ree and come to tea. Wherever my finger drops in the yellow pages, I call the number listed to ask about the services that company offers. For example, I've learned about the skunk patrol, tubular skylight installation, and all-night discount dentistry. A recording sings, "One two three. The fourth is free." Y'couldn't make this up.

Gathering this information makes me think about new things. It cranks up my curiosity and lets me use new words I don't get to sing in songs. It's an adventure that just takes a few minutes, it's free, legal, and down the road, if my stuffed bear ever needs a facelift, I'll know who to call.

RE-ROUTE

For a quick exercise out of the house, next time you're headed somewhere you go every day, take the long way. You'll see different cars, different children leaving school with their colorful backpacks, new street signs like detour, closed 'til 5/27. Slow traffic. Tree trimming. Slow down and yield.

I could write a silly song about each of those street signs. So can you. Try it.

NEW TRANSPORTATION

Next time your car's in the shop, instead of bemoaning your lack of wheels for the day, take a bus. In Los Angeles that comes under the heading of science-fiction. Truthfully, we usually just rent another car. But I tried it. Taking the bus, you're coming face to face with people you wouldn't ordinarily meet. Observe them. Do they wear glasses? What kind? What color? Hats? Backpacks? Do the other passengers have bus passes? Is someone a little short on "exact change only"? Be the one who "finds some coins on the floor" and gives them to that unfortunate rider. What languages do your fellow passengers speak? Survey their shoes. All sneakers? What brands? Colors? Holes? How many riders are wearing headphones?

This experience gave me a whole new vocabulary to work with. I also wondered how many hours the lady with the Target badge had worked that day so her kids could have a better life.

I don't remember why, but back in the day, I borrowed my neighbor's pickup. Driving it after my Rabbit convertible was astounding. Riding up that high made me feel like a trucker. I assumed a different persona. Molly Belle, the singing teamster, was on her way to Chattanooga with a load of beets. Driving like a lunatic, almost no lives were lost, and it was an adventure. The best part was having a lot of new thoughts swirling around me. Molly Belle tried something new, loved it, and got home pumped up, ready to write.

If I were a semi.

While my foot was in a big black boot and healing from surgery, I bought a three-wheeled red scooter. For a person who is meticulous about keeping her car in perfect condition, it was fun and a delightful departure to zip around my house, crashing into walls. My handyman built me a ramp at the back door, so I was able to escape onto our winding street lined with blooming Jacaranda trees. While their flowers sprinkled down on me like lavender fairy dust, I beeped my horn with the kids on their bikes, passed nannies pushing designer babies in designer strollers, zigged and zagged through the parade of dog walkers, and for the first time, noticed parked orange smart cars with expired plates from Suriname.

This was a major change of pace from driving down the same street in my seventh white car in a row, same brand, heading to the same places. Although I don't recommend you have foot surgery, rockin' that scooter gave me insight into life lower to the ground, plus a lot of new, playful sights and adventures. It took me away from my "shoulds," I made new friends, and I had fun, which, more than anything, inspires a writer full of possibilities to run to the keyboard.

PHYSICAL EXERCISE

Since writing is cerebral, doing something physical works wonders for stimulating creativity. Some people jog or walk every morning. While doing that, and perspiring, their whole bodies are invigorated. When they're exercising, these people forget the lists of things they have to do and focus on putting one foot in front of the other. Their objective is to complete their two or five miles, or even just getting to the mailbox at the corner. They have short-term goals that are physically demanding but quite easily accomplished. When they finish, it's a victory. And a win is a guaranteed catalyst to put the tush in the chair.

When I do my exercise, I usually feel a sense of completion and pride and can then move on to the next task at hand: writing. To warm up, I may write a silly song:

> I ran five miles
> You ran five miles
> They ran four
> We ee ee eee eee ran more.

Accomplishing something physical early in your day is a great way of creating momentum for cerebral exercise later. Completing one thing gives you courage and incentive to start another.

On days when I have zero energy, I talk to myself like I'm five. "Why don't we just do this one little load of laundry, then go back to the couch and watch the French Open? With oatmeal cookies. Wanna try that?"

Dirty laundry goes into the washing machine. Clean laundry comes out. Something happened. I did it. That gives me courage to try something else that's easy, but which I hate. Like emptying the dishwasher. Then I'm rolling and may even start folding my clean clothes. When that's finished, I might segue into actually sitting at my desk "for five minutes" and see what happens there, during the French Open commercials. Without the demand to win Grammys, ideas float in and dance around my desk.

Or, to tease yourself into putting words on paper, say you'll only try for four and a half minutes. Then, there's no demand for it to be brilliant. You promised yourself words, you didn't say anything about them having to be good ones. I mean what could you possibly do in four and a half minutes to change the world? Y'never know. Just do it.

MEDITATING

Midway through my day, I feel scrunched from difficult phone calls and texts, along with emails like the ones demanding I hand over Taylor Swift's private cell phone number or someone will blow up my house. Saying that Taylor recently changed her number and hasn't given me the new one yet rarely works.

So I shut down my computer, turn off my cell phone, hide it in the freezer, lay my yoga mat under the pink bougainvillea on my patio, and meditate with the seagulls for fifteen minutes. For the first five, I trace a circle with a dot in the middle on my leg. After that, the shape becomes two intersecting lines, with the dot where they meet. That morphs into a triangle with a dot in the middle for the last five minutes. If my mind wanders, I keep on tracing my shapes, which brings me back in. And when my fifteen minutes are up, I feel completely refreshed, peaceful, thank myself and the universe, make myself an apple-peach-banana smoothie, and go back to work.

If you don't meditate, please try for two minutes. If that doesn't work, try it again the next day. As you slowly release control and let yourself get into the mindset of only seeing white space instead of your list of a hundred shoulds, you're on your way to creating tranquility when the day is cranky and getting worse.

GETTING UNSTUCK CHECKLIST

Did you do any exercise today?

Meditate?

Practice yoga?

Did you play the yellow pages game?

Did you take a bus or other form of public transportation?

Did you drive down a different street, shop at a different market, go to a new dry cleaner?

Did you talk to a stranger? Make up a new persona while doing so?

Did you go to a museum?

Did you write a nonsense song?

Did you peruse a newspaper or magazine you normally don't read?

If you get all noes, choose a couple of items in the list above and do them. If you get all yeses and you're still stuck, I think you definitely need to fall in love. If that still doesn't give you grist for the mill, break up. THIS will do it. You can take THAT to the bank.

YOGA

I started practicing yoga after all the stretch classes were canceled at Equinox on Sepulveda in LA, because yoga was trendy. Swell. I attended grudgingly because I didn't think I could do those elaborate moves like the rubber band women who weighed ninety-nine pounds. I mean hey, I've never been to an ashram and I'm prone to altitude sickness, so I'd never survive in the Himalayas, and I didn't especially care for that purple yoga mat color. But I had an expensive membership and my body needed to be stretched. So I hid in the back corner of the studio and tried.

Son of a gun! In addition to getting a wonderful workout, I found that as I did the yoga poses, and especially the breathing, for the hour or so I was in the class, I was really thinking about yoga and nothing else. That's unusual for me and my "monkey mind" that's racing and bouncing off ninety-three things at once. But in the yoga studio, I honestly felt I was present.

Additionally, no matter how long I've been stuck on a song, the word or thought I need often floats in while I'm downward dogging or saluting the sun. That's because I'm completely relaxed and open to the to the blessings of the universe.

If you're not yet a yogi or yogini, I urge you to try a beginner class or two, unless the instructor insists on playing that mellifluous "I am a hyena being sawed in half" torture music, so popular on the central coast of California these days. Jesus. In the first class I attended, while our instructor was in a trance, I sneaked up to the front of the room and disconnected the speakers. I mean, really. You can't do that to my ears.

No matter what is going on in my life, I make time for my daily practice. And I'm beyond grateful for the peace I find, and especially the positive energy I am able to unleash and take home with me.

In our chaotic world, where I'm actually afraid to turn on the news, nothing is more important for me, and you, as artists, than to feel peace and positive energy. Without it, there wouldn't be any songs at all.

During my career as a tunesmith, I've learned that hit songs are often hiding in stretched muscles. You can take that to the bank.

Try it.

THE MAGIC OF WRITING CHILDREN'S MUSIC

INTERVIEW WITH GRAMMY AND EMMY-AWARD WINNERS MICHAEL SILVERSHER AND PATTY SILVERSHER

Michael Silversher and Patty Silversher have been writing together for thirty-one years. They've had an astonishing career that gets better every day. While the rest of us were chasing pop hits, Michael and Patty were quietly writing for the children's marketplace. And Michael told me they've never run after work. It always comes to them.

When Michael was eight, he was inspired by Alfred Newman's score to *The President's Lady* and wanted to write in that moody genre. Soon after, he composed a song with his first lyric, about his sister's painting of a rock, and called it "Wasted Man," as wasted as a man could be at eight years old.

When I asked Patty what her dream was when starting out as a songwriter, she said that initially she didn't have one. A psychology major, she was just living in her sorority house, strumming a little guitar, and loved to play with words. Then she met

Michael, who had written a Christmas song for a contest. She boldly told him, "I think I'm gonna change the lyric," did so, and they won first prize for "Christmas in My Heart."

At the time, they were living in Palo Alto, California. Michael was the assistant manager of a musical instrument shop. At night, he sneaked in with his old reel-to-reel machine to record his new material, using all the instruments in the store. Patty was a waitress at Good Earth, frequented by Steve Jobs, known to be nasty, and never, ever leaving a tip. As snarly and disrespectful as Jobs was to Patty, she gave it right back to him, and when he finished his meal, he slapped a twenty-dollar tip on his table.

That was perfect training for the music business. Y'want something done—y'ask Patty. Period.

She and Michael founded the Northern California Songwriters Association. Soon after, Michael wrote "The Whole World Sounds Like Michael McDonald," which everyone at the Songwriter's meeting loved. Patty raced their recording right over to a local radio station, where the song was played and played, and the switchboard lit up for days requesting that tune.

Soon after, at an ASCAP conference in LA, Disney's Tom Bocci heard the Michael McDonald song and asked the Silvershers to submit material to him for their *Mousercise* album. Bocci accepted their song "Pig Out," and the album went platinum.

Meanwhile, Michael was signed to do a movie based on the life of Harvey Milk. The same week, Yamaha gave him $30,000 worth of synthesizers as a Writer in Residence.

He said, "I started messing around, doing demos for Disney, and they asked me to produce their next album. It sold four hundred thousand copies. Patty and I had eight songs on that one. Disney kept hiring us to create tunes for their storybooks, which were forty-fives with songs on one side and stories on the other. Some titles were 'Just Me and My Dad,' as well as 'Just

Gramma and Me.' I was the voice of Little Critter." And Patty added, "My sneeze was the page turner. Every time I sneezed, the kids knew to turn the page."

Another project was *Rainbow Brite*, a joint venture between Disney and Hallmark. "It featured our song 'A Rainbow in Your Heart,'" Michael said proudly, "and I was the voice of Twink, a fuzzy white creature.

"It was a huge kids' project," he added. "After that, Disney approached the biggest rock stars to create songs for it, giving them six weeks to produce their original material. Often, when Disney didn't accept it, they came running to us, needing a three-day turnaround."

Patty and Michael were on a roll, writing theme songs for Disney TV shows, including *Gummi Bears* and *Tailspin*. Those songs are available now on YouTube, in dozens of languages.

After writing "Perfect Tree," for Jim Henson's *Mr. Willowby's Christmas Tree*, starring Robert Downey Jr., "We continued working with Henson's company. I was spitting out lyrics," Patty told me. "We wrote seventy songs for them. They gave us an office on La Brea, which was Charlie Chaplin's former studio. We were assigned to the costume vault. Nobody knew the combination to it, so we couldn't lock the door. But there we were, on campus. When we'd write something, we'd run down the hall, grab listeners from wardrobe and plumbing, they'd say yeah or nay. We were part of the creation of the whole thing."

What did they do when the music wasn't flowing and they were stuck? Michael laughed. "We drove over to the Glendale Mall, wandering around in the white noise. Everything I heard that rose above the white noise was something I could use."

I asked Patty, if she could take a long walk through a spring forest with any composer, songwriter, or musician, who would it be?

"Dolly Parton. I'm mostly Motown, but she's a fascinating person."

Michael's answer to the same question was George Gershwin.

I also asked the Silvershers which song they'd each take to rock 'n' roll Heaven, to show St. Peter they spent their lives well. Patty's response was "Places in the Heart." Michael agreed. "We wrote that one just after my dad died. I dedicated it to him, and the song was nominated for a Primetime Emmy."

My final question was this: If you were standing at the mike, onstage, and the entire world was watching you—all seven billion souls—and you had a few seconds to say something before the world ended, what would it be?

Patty said, "I'd sing 'Places in the Heart,' a cappella.[1]"

And Michael would sing "A Simple Prayer.[2]"

I'm proud to know Patty and Michael. Their writing sings for itself.

---

1   https://www.youtube.com/watch?v=36_07v8U6LQ&ab_channel=AndrewsMagicandMore

2   https://soundcloud.com/bill-cuomo/a-simple-prayer

CHAPTER 8

OVERCOMING WRITING BLOCKS

Oscar-winning screenwriter Frank Pierson, and president of the Academy of Motion Picture Arts and Sciences, was a breakfast buddy at Marjan's Deli in LA's Brentwood Country Mart. I used to observe his extraordinary life every morning and wonder how to get from my bowl of oatmeal to his. Right after I'd been nominated for an Emmy, I was blocked. I couldn't even write a check. Would he help me get through it?

Frank slammed down his coffee cup and told me he didn't believe in writer's block. "Y'get drunk, get laid, and get back to work." It worked for him. Frank didn't acknowledge writer's block. Period. My tall, elegant friend, whom everyone mistook for Hemingway, just bullied his way through it.

No writer, no matter how famous, honored, prolific, rich, adored, quoted, industrious, or disciplined, hasn't faced the terror of feeling stuck. There is nothing as devastating or debilitating as that sickening feeling. It's like taking a euphoric glider flight over a yellow meadow and then suddenly being pushed from 20,000 feet without a parachute onto the terrain below, which has somehow morphed into sheet rock.

I've been there. I've gotten through it. I've been back and lived to tell about it, proudly showing off the new songs I've penned after the battles were over. If I can nurture myself through that agony, so can you.

WHAT CAUSES WRITER'S BLOCK?

Writer's block is caused by fear or anger or both. Every dry spell in my life can be traced back to one or the other. It's as though they go out for a drink and leave you there in a puddle of screaming mush, wondering what the heck happened. You were doing so well this morning! You feel frantic, doomed. You are lost forever. You're never going to write again. Your only hope and salvation is a real job with no demands. Just show up at nine, leave at five. You're not a writer anymore. It's over. Forever. Amen.

Does any of this sound familiar? I bet it does. You might have seen me online, searching furiously through the Indeed.com site, noting the listings for slugs. Maybe you've seen the new GRE study guide on my desk, as I plan to get a PhD and a real life. Or perhaps you've hacked my credit card and saw my purchase of a dozen how-to books containing strategies to earn $1,000,000 a month selling virtual yaks in my spare time. Or did you, perhaps, catch my act as I scoured every publication from *Barron's* to *The Wall Street Journal*, foraging for a kind, heterosexual, single tycoon to take me off my own failed hands, marry me, and enjoy this poetry/ditty thing I've got going.

I'm in good company. Every successful writer has crashed into this abyss. On dark, stuck days I see the shadow of Stephen Foster across the street, climbing the blue oleander bushes, preparing to jump in front of a Big Blue Santa Monica bus careening down the Berkeley Street hill. I swear I saw Shakespeare in holey sweats at Inspiration Point along the ocean, ripping pages out of his notebook and muttering to himself like a bag lady. It's entirely possible for a songwriter who won a Grammy last year to be unable to scribble a note for his cleaning lady now. Crazed, he grabs his award and heads for the trash bin.

But a kid on a skateboard whizzes by, whistling a tune our songwriter wrote, and the crisis is over. A little recognition makes it all go away. The tunesmith races home, back to his piano, where he proudly replaces his trophy on top, and begins to feel the new feelings float from the universe through his fingers onto the black and white keys.

A poet I used to know, who lived on donations from lonely housewives in Beverly Hills, says he writes about being stuck. I tried it, and it worked.

OVERCOMING WRITER'S BLOCK EXERCISE

The best possible remedy for being blocked is doing physical exercise. Run five miles. Or two. Work out for an hour. Stretch afterwards, for fifteen minutes. Take a shower. All pumped up emotionally, and cleansed physically, I bet you'll feel empowered to write something down. I always do.

Try it.

I take long walks—sometimes through a nearby woodsy park, where a creek flows by. In this rural environment, I'm pumped full of oxygen from the exercise, and the fresh air is exhilarating. As I round the path for home, ideas are running behind me, calling out, "Hey, Molly," begging me to write them down. And when I get home, I grab my pen, save them all, and wonder which song to write first.

NURTURE YOURSELF

What would you do if you saw a barefoot, freckle-faced, four-year-old kid in a gold Lakers t-shirt and a blue Dodgers cap sobbing on your doorstep? His ice cream fell out of the sugar cone onto the sidewalk. Wouldn't you want to comfort him?

I'd hug him, rock him in my rocking chair, maybe lend him my teddy bear, kiss him on the forehead, gently squeeze his hand, and tell him it's all gonna be okay. I'd buy him another ice cream cone, with two scoops. We'd go to a toy store where I'd tell him he could have anything he wanted—absolutely anything. I'd tell him a story I make up on the spot and remind him over and over how special he is. I'd pamper him. I'd protect him. I'd surprise him and make this the best day of his life.

Each of us has a lost, needy four-year-old inside of us when we are blocked on what I call midnight afternoons. I want you to make a list of twenty things about your unhappy little person. Describe him or her in precise detail.

Here are some questions to ask yourself to get you started:

> Hair color? Curly or straight?
>
> Eye color?
>
> Missing teeth?
>
> Which ones?
>
> Skinny? Chubby?
>
> Scab on the knee? From what?
>
> Which languages does he speak? Does he lisp?
>
> Where is his family?
>
> Did an older kid steal his baseball cards?

Keep going. List ten more things about this sad, little person.

When you're finished, you'll see how needy this kid is and how loving you can be, making it all up to him.

This child is you. So take care of and comfort yourself just as you would this unhappy little person. Make a list of twenty things you can do to pamper yourself, then do them. If you can learn to do that, you will know how to take care of the frightened child inside you and make yourself feel safe again.

People who feel safe can move on. They can take chances with blank pages. People who feel safe with blank pages are pumped from knowing their ideas are good, and they write them down. People with good ideas written down find better ones and eventually discover a great one they want to run with. They nurture it, tweak it, refine it, rewrite it, and finish it. Then most important, they reward themselves for their victory.

With that momentum, they write something else and something else.

See? Start slowly. Keep going. You can do it.

PRODUCTION MUSIC JACKPOT

INTERVIEW WITH ART MUNSON, CREATOR/PRODUCER

Art and I were staff writers at Almo Music. From the get-go, I could tell he was enormously creative, commercial, and an amazing instrumentalist. Give him any guitar, bass, mandolin, banjo—he's a virtuoso—and he plays "just enough piano to be dangerous." Lucky for me, we wrote a few good songs together, including "I Hit the Jackpot." Even though he was usually on the road in the Paul Williams's Good Shepherd Quintet, he'd call me from payphones in Indiana, Arkansas, and Idaho, and we'd collaborate that way between his gigs.

After his deal ended with Almo, Art set up a studio in his home called Art's House. All of us on-the-cusp songwriters recorded our new material there. We could always count on Art for the latest equipment, plus his great ears.

In addition to running the studio, Art was an entrepreneur. He smartly invested in real estate. Other than owning the big white house in Los Feliz where the Manson Family murdered his tenants, he did very well. Art continued to write while he bought and sold property. So his mortgage was always paid, no matter what was or wasn't happening in the music business. But a musician has to musish.

Art was always one step ahead of the music marketplace and stumbled on a need for used DATs (Digital Audio Tapes) by Deadheads. At one point, he actually made a great living selling them, by the case, to fans of that band who never had enough copies of enough concerts.

Go figure.

But he missed making music. And since his previous songwriting doors were no longer open, he figured out a way to write and produce production music for TV shows, and, ultimately, have those tracks support him.

As always, his compositions have his special fingerprint on them. Before they're even written, they have homes. Few composers can say that about their work. Now Art is able to do what few creative people in the world can do: create the music he loves to write and live well on his royalties plus license fees.

His breakthrough in writing tracks for TV shows came when he and his wife were at a party. An acquaintance of theirs had been dating someone who worked at a music production company and was complaining about the quality of the music they were getting for their shows. "He mentioned me, and I started writing for them. They were all on HGTV at first, the makeover shows, like *Save My Bath* and *Spice Up My Kitchen*."

His music has also been featured on *The Voice*, ABC News, *Property Brothers: Forever Home*, *American Picker*, and many more. Most recently he had a nice placement with a SingleCare commercial that featured Martin Sheen. That ran for a year and has turned into some nice royalties.

I asked Art if there's one track he's especially proud to have written. "We love all our children," he replied. But although he receives royalties from BMI and license fees, his name does not appear in the credits. That's a decision each songwriter has to make for himself.

How does Art know how much to charge? "What I feel is fair. Most of the income is from royalties. License fees from *traditional* music libraries can be quite a bit higher, in the thousands of dollars."

Did he ever miss having all the best songwriters, singers, and musicians in his studio? "Not at all. My control freak nature enjoys working alone or with my wife. There are so many software tools now, and with my musical background, I can write just about anything."

When I asked Art what he hasn't done yet as a composer/producer/songwriter that's still on his bucket list, his answer was, "having a hit record. Isn't that what we all really want? Truthfully, it wouldn't make me any happier or more fulfilled than I already am."

My final question was, what would he be doing if he wasn't a musician?

"Tending my garden."

Isn't that energy the same?

CHAPTER 9

GETTING READY TO WRITE

Too many tunesmiths misinterpret their pre-writing phase as writer's block. However, they're simply getting ready to write.

I want you to be good to yourselves and recognize your own, personal, eccentric, and in my case, wonky, warm-up. Here's what I do:

I locate my heating pad and put it on my bed at precisely the right angle.

I arrange my two writing pillows behind my back, just so.

I place my thesaurus and rhyming dictionary exactly at arm's length.

I place my title book and current, college-lined notebook right next to the thesaurus.

I get up to make myself a cup of honey vanilla chamomile tea.

I get up again to find myself something to dunk in my honey vanilla chamomile tea.

I make myself another cup of tea that doesn't have cookie crumbs in it.

I search for my mp3 player.

Then I hunt down the other mp3 player.

But I don't have my lucky pen.

That takes another ten minutes. Or an hour.

But then I remember the 10¢ off coupon about to expire for tea bags on sale eighteen miles away. I take the long way home, with my mp3 blasting, boil the water for another cup of tea, then decide on a can of ginger ale instead.

Early in my songwriting career, I used to make myself crazy with negative rants about all the prime time I was wasting while going through each of these steps and not writing. But I finally discovered all of those distractions were really parts of the warm-up process I needed to go through before I felt safe enough to scribble something down.

By the way, until I'm rolling, I don't write on the lines in my notebook. Instead, I jot down ideas and phrases in the corners of pages, across the middle on an angle or in teeny print along the edges. But when I get a jolt and love something, ah ha, THEN I take a deep breath and use the real lines on my pages.

During this eccentric process, instead of beating myself up about NOT writing, I gently assure me I'm warming up. Like a tennis player at Wimbledon. Overheads. Serves. Backhands, cross court shots. Up to the net. Back to the baseline. When I'm ready, look out. Here comes Molly with her sharp pencil.

Other seemingly dumb stuff I do to warm up:

Before a writing session, I hand wash my dishes. Why don't I just use the dishwasher? The warm soapy water feels good and it's sensuous at the same time. I take a dirty dish, scrub it, then it's clean. I did that. I control it. I have momentum. Momentum from one activity leads to another. If this happens for me, it will for you too. So find your version of washing dishes.

LOOSENING UP EXERCISE

Make a list of all the things you did before you last had a productive writing session. Don't leave anything out, even making love or taking a shower or doing a push up while making love in the shower. Keep one important thing in mind. You didn't get blocked overnight. And you might not get unblocked that quickly either. You have to work through it. Give yourself the time to do that. I know you're impatient and wanna wanna wanna get back to work—now! However, if you really intend to solve this problem, give it time. By putting too great a demand on unblocking, you're just creating a new series of frustrations.

IT MIGHT BE FEAR

When you're stuck, make a list of things that frighten you. I'm talking about what might happen if the BIG Earthquake rattles your home into designer dust. Or if the stock market crashes? Come on. You're a neurotic writer. There must be something you're afraid might happen.

Make a detailed list of everything you're "a-scared of" as my goddaughter would say. Nobody but you will see that list. Nobody's going to laugh at you or tell you to up your meds.

Here are some questions to get you started:

Is there something you have to do that makes you a little uneasy?

Did somebody you don't even know say something flippantly that caught you off guard and made you question your ability to create original songs?

Do you think your career has peaked?

Are you worried about earning a living?

Did someone imply you're just another hack and in no way unique?

Did he say it in jest but do you now wonder if he wasn't kidding?

Do you worry that your friends are doing better than you are?

If you're a writer with a contract or assignment, do you think your publisher won't like what you create and terminate you?

Do you think you'll be bought out of your contract and dumped?

Do you worry they'll hire someone younger and smarter in your place?

Then beside each item on your list, write a reply, soothing your fears. Rally for yourself. Be bold. Be brave. Trample the bad stuff coming to flatten you. Be nurturing and loving.

IT MIGHT BE ANGER

If you're blocked and you're not afraid, then by process of elimination, you're angry. It will help you get to the source if you ask yourself these questions:

Are you furious, totally aggravated, mildly disturbed, some-what annoyed? How about your neighbor who parks his car too close to yours and dings your showroom-new doors?

What happened last week that still has you grinding your teeth? Here's your chance to punch its lights out.

As sensitive people, we tunesmiths wound easily. As artists, we're missing the top layer of our skin, so we react immediately—no protection, no filter.

I want you to describe your rage. Pick up your pen and scribble whatever is growling inside in the form of a letter—a letter you aren't ever going to mail. You can use as many four-letter words as you want. Never mind punctuation either. Squeeze it out of your gut. If writing by hand or computer doesn't do it for you, scream into an mp3 player, then play it back, loud, as you purge your soul of vicious clog.

People who are free of anger can feel gentle things. When we're happy, we can let go and allow good things to happen to us. When we're not angry anymore, we have time to feel some-thing else and do something else. We can refocus our energy and find some new magic out there. You may "get" two words that usually don't go together that might make a good song title. Then other phrases float in. Pretty soon you have several scribbles that could grow up to be a song. You move the words around a little and you've got an explosive title. You make a note of everything. And what do y'know, you're writing again.

CHANGE YOUR WARDROBE

When I have a creative date with me, I usually pull on old grey sweats that are so worn, I can see through them. By the end of the day there are cookie crumbs all down the front. My usually perfect hair looks nuked, and the mascara from the previous evening is somewhere down around my chin. There's even a hole in my lucky lavender socks.

But on those days when I don't feel like writing or looking that unsavory, I warm up by washing my hair and styling it just so. I choose my favorite eye shadow combination, unwrap a new pair of fancy pantyhose and put them on with the new outfit I've been saving for a special occasion. Then I make a deal with myself to go into my office for five minutes—just five—to tidy up some papers. Before I know it, I'm sitting at my desk, for—okay—five more minutes, but that's it—and loving it. What this amounts to is making a happy occasion out of writing instead of the same old monotonous shivering "should" festival. Celebrate your commitment to your craft and see how happy you feel.

Whether you're blocked or simply have a long warm-up process, I hope you realize now that it's perfectly natural for you to take side roads and detours to get to your work destination mindset. I don't care if you could have gone from A to B in three seconds if you went from A to Z then back to B via Z. Give yourself permission to indulge in your warm-up time. Once you complete it, your writing will come a lot easier and more playfully because you'll be in a much more positive frame of mind when you start. That can only lead to more positive results.

Try it.

And hang your process on the refrigerator door for safe-keeping. Then it'll be there whenever you need it.

Honest.

THE POWER OF MUSIC SUPERVISION

INTERVIEW WITH ROBIN URDANG, EMMY AWARD–WINNING MUSIC SUPERVISOR

As a music supervisor, Robin's credits fill two single-spaced, double-sided pages, and include three Primetime Emmys for *The Marvelous Mrs. Maisel*. I asked her these questions.

ML: What does a music supervisor do?

RU: Every project is different, as is every music supervisor, and how they approach the job. But a general answer is this: a music supervisor oversees all aspects of the music for a project to make sure that the director's and producer's vision is being realized. Music plays a huge role in all visual media and can enhance the storyline and work to perfection or not work well at all, which is damaging the project. A music supervisor pitches music, oversees on-camera performances, clears the songs and negotiates the fees, hires the composer, and many procure the soundtrack deal as well.

ML: Do you have final say on the music you include in each episode's soundtrack?

RU: Definitely not. All I can do is suggest and pitch and give my opinion. The final decision comes down to the filmmaker.

ML: Is there a course or class to take to become a music supervisor?

RU: UCLA has one.

ML: How did you break into the business?

RU: I started by working in a music management company in New York, then an agency and a promotion company. I moved to Los Angeles, where I continued in the same path, which ultimately lead me to a position on *The Mambo Kings*, a film with Antonio Banderas. It shot in New York so I went back there to work with Robert Kraft, who was the Executive Music Producer.

I learned so much about music and film, on camera production, clearances, and more from him. I started getting hired to work on independent pictures and studio films that had a lot of on-camera performances. Back in Los Angeles, I started my own company and began working all of the time. Eventually, I broke into television, with the show *Burn Notice* and then *Brothers and Sisters*. Some of the films and shows I got were based on relationships I had with one of the filmmakers, and from there, my career kept moving forward.

ML: How do songwriters get past your gatekeepers to pitch their tracks for your projects?

RU: Most songwriters send emails. It's hit or miss. I may be looking for music, I may not. But, if the music is tagged properly with metadata and a link is sent, it will normally go in my "independent music" file.

ML: What are some of your favorite projects?

RU: *The Marvelous Mrs. Maisel*, *Call Me by Your Name*, *Younger*, *Burn Notice* (my first TV series), *We Are Who We Are* (current TV series), and *Adam* (an independent film that I think was so beautiful).

ML: How did you get those gigs?

RU: For *The Marvelous Mrs. Maisel*, I was brought in by the production company for Bun Heads, that Amy Sherman-Palladino and Dan Palladino were creators, writers, directors on. I had a meeting, got the gig, and have worked with them ever since. I'm grateful and love working with them. We have the most exceptional team, which starts from the top.

For Luca Guadagnino's projects (*We Are Who We Are, Call Me by Your Name, Suspiria*), I was brought on to the film, *A Bigger Splash*, by Michael Costigan, a producer I had worked with years earlier on *Glitter*. Luca and I bonded immediately. We have worked with Michael on every project since. He is genius, and I adore working with him.

Adam was my sister Leslie Urdang's film. She hired me and has hired me on everything since. I've worked on some beautiful films of hers. *Beginners, Rabbit Hole, The Seagull*, and currently working on *Wild Mountain Thyme* (directed by John Patrick Shanley). I have to say that meeting Christopher Plummer (Captain von Trapp) on *Beginners* was one of the highlights of my life. My favorite film is *The Sound of Music*.

ML: Does a music supervisor need an agent, like a composer?

RU: I presume if a person doesn't have contacts and is not comfortable pitching themselves or negotiating, an agent is helpful. I don't have one. I'm sure if I did, I'd get paid better.

ML: What are the current rates paid for usage of music in an episode? Feature?

RU: It varies on what it is. Music can cost anywhere from $500 to hundreds of thousands. I'd say on average, around $20,000–$50,000 per song for TV. And a bit higher for film.

ML: On what new platforms do you think music will be available after streaming?

RU: I haven't any idea. I'm still figuring out all the tech platforms now.

ML: Songwriters and artists are having a very hard time now that so much of their work is pirated. What do you foresee happening to our rights and royalties?

RU: I think we still need to fight for the royalties and rights to stay with the songwriters, and publishers have to help. Like anything else, we have to change as things evolve and new media comes in to play. Unions help.

ML: Where do you look for new writers and artists?

RU: Radio, labels, publishers, indie companies, and indie artists send me music all of the time. And, online research.

ML: Do you hold pitch sessions?

RU: No.

ML: With your special gifts, do you do something as a music supervisor that nobody else does?

RU: I don't know what special gifts I have. I just work hard and am honest about what I can and can't do, what I can afford to pay for songs and what I can't. I try and be fair and upfront with clearance companies. Creatively, we all have our own taste, but ultimately, it is the music that works in the picture that gets chosen. (Or, we hope it does.) I don't always like the songs I choose, or the style of music, but it's not what my personal music taste is. I have turned down films or TV shows if I don't like the subject matter or think I will have a hard time listening to the music. I think every music supervisor has their own way of working. I do, at least, have the experience of every aspect of what a music supervisor can do. I used to say, my two-or-three-person company is like its own mini music department.

ML: What steps would you suggest to a person wanting your job, to break into your profession?

RU: Understand that it is not only about the music and how big a record collection you have. There are a lot of nuts and bolts to deal with. Work for a music supervisor, intern for one. Then you will know if it is something you want to pursue or not. I have had interns/ assistants/coordinators that have learned so much and also learned where they wanted to be next—a record label, a film studio, a trailer house, or completely out of the business. I highly recommend finding a well-established "sup" to at least intern for. Also, join the Guild of Music Supervisors, watch the panels discussions, read, and go to the workshops.

ML: How did you prepare for your profession?

RU: I didn't. I fell into it. I'm a good multi-tasker, love music, and worked hard. I studied psychology, which I think should be a pre-requisite for this business.

ML: What would you like to bring to music supervising that isn't there now?

RU: Maybe an easy way to lay music into picture without having to learn the music editing end.

CHAPTER 10

ROYALTIES

While attempting to contact all the performing rights societies for typical royalties now, paid for various kinds of music and song performances, every dead end smashed into me. Twice. Nobody would tell me anything. Hissy board members hung up on me. Executives I've worked with all my life wouldn't divulge specifics. What? I'm not some bowlegged, schlock scammer selling third mortgages on pink igloos in Medicine Hat, but I felt like it. Then, God bless composer Richard Bellis for suggesting I contact the Brabecs.

I remember meeting Todd and Jeff Brabec during my first visit to ASCAP back in the day, when I was driving a dented, used, red VW bug with a leaky sunroof up and down Sunset Boulevard in Hollywood looking for my shot. Handsome twins and lawyers, the Brabecs are dedicated to helping songwriters and composers succeed.

Their book, *Music, Money and Success,* is a tome we all need on our desks to refer to when a legal question comes up and we need the real answer, not a guess from some yutz on the internet posing as an attorney who studied law for fun and profit on a matchbook from Jiggles strip club.

Todd and Jeff graciously sent me a copy of the eighth edition of their book and gave me permission to use parts of it to share with you, here.

So—where do our royalties come from?

According to the Brabecs, most of the money that we earn as songwriters comes from the performing rights area. There are organizations that collect royalties for us in the USA and in foreign countries throughout the rest of the world. These organizations represent most songwriters, film and TV composers, and music publishers.

The performing rights societies are: the American Society of Composers, Authors, and Publishers (ASCAP), Broadcast Music, Inc. (BMI), SESAC (the Society of European Stage Authors and Composers), and Global Music Rights (GMR).

Together, those four societies collect more than seven billion dollars for us a year. Beats workin'.

Performance royalty income continues well beyond the lives of many writers. In fact, the copyright for our work is the life of the writer plus seventy years.

Though the royalty figures vary for any given type of use, based on many factors, table 10.1 from the Brabecs' book below shows you the type of monies that can be earned in this field

1. Number One *Billboard* pop song of the year: Writer and publisher income: $2,400,000

2. Ten minutes of underscore per episode on a network TV series airing for ten years: Writer and publisher income: $1,656,000

3. Theme song for a network TV series on the air for five years: $460,000

4. Song performed on a primetime network TV: $7,000

5. Hit song used in a commercial with a two-year broadcast run: $400,000

6. Number one pop chart single: $1,400,000

7. Number ten pop chart single: $500,000

8. Number fifty pop chart single: $90,000

9. Fifteen minutes of underscore on each episode of a television series airing for one year: $44,000

10. One performance of a primetime network television series theme song: $2,000

11. A major popular song's lifetime of copyright earnings: $7,000,000

12. Jingle performance on network television: fifty dollars

13. Production company logo: fifty dollars

14. Worldwide foreign performances of a top ten chart hit: $1,600,000

15. One college radio performance: six cents

16. Foreign performances of the underscore from a number one worldwide blockbuster movie: $1,000,000

INCOME FOR MUSIC PUBLISHERS AND SONGWRITERS

Here's a list of sources for songwriter and publishing royalties:

1. Performing rights payments (performances for profit)
2. CD and record sales (mechanical income)
3. Downloads
4. Mechanical licenses
5. Television series
6. Motion pictures
7. Home video/personal video/DVDs/Blu-ray/downloads
8. Commercials (fees for using hit songs range from $75,000 to $1,000,000)
9. Video games
10. Karaoke/sing-alongs
11. Internet karaoke sites
12. Video jukeboxes
13. Lyric reprints in novels or nonfiction books
14. Lyric reprints in magazines
15. Monthly song, lyric, and sheet music magazines
16. Public service announcements
17. Records of hit songs with changed lyrics
18. Medleys
19. Promotional videos
20. Greeting cards
21. Musical greeting cards

22. Electronic greeting cards

23. Television commercials for motion pictures

24. Home and personal video (TV programs)

25. Home and personal video (recording artists)

26. Foreign theatrical royalties (motion pictures)

27. Dolls and toys

28. Television programs and motion pictures based on songs

29. Books based on motion pictures (lyric reprints)

30. Books about a lyricist

31. Remixes

32. Novelty and theme song albums

33. Lyrics on albums, downloads, and CD packages

34. Sheet music and folios

35. Television and motion picture background scores

36. Lyrics and music on soda cans

37. Lyrics on merchandise

38. Lyrics on t-shirts, clothing, and posters

39. Lyrics on direct-to-consumer merchandise

40. Audio records of books

41. Special products albums

42. TV sale–only albums

43. Key outlet marketing albums

44. Bonus and hidden tracks on an album

45. Limited edition collectibles

46. Musical telephones
47. Singing fish
48. Theme parks
49. Ringtones
50. Compilation albums/mechanical rates based on past success
51. Musical door chimes
52. Musical candles
53. Musical flowers
54. Corporate in-house videos
55. Music boxes
56. Slot machines
57. Musical instrument toys
58. Background music services
59. Internet musical instrument lessons
60. Physical coins
61. Holograms
62. Menu screens
63. Co-branding videos
64. Virtual reality
65. Sampling

"I HAVE MY OWN PUBLISHING COMPANY"

A big mistake many songwriters, lyricists, bands, and composers make is insisting on having their own music publishing companies. Whenever someone tells me of this plan, I ask them these four questions:

1. Do you have any meaningful contacts in the real music business?

2. Do you know anybody at a legitimate label offering you a deal?

3. Do you have any experience in business?

4. Are you a good hustler, goin' after it 24/7?

In the case of all the above answers being negative, the writers with their own publishing own 100 percent of nothing.

With the pieces of the songwriting pie getting smaller, labels, managers, and agents are incentivized by getting as big a slice of your deal as possible. If it's between signing you, who has no publishing to offer, or Mackie Z, with 100 percent of his publishing to offer, who's going to get the deal? Not you.

Early in my career, my mentor told me that lots of songwriters with great material have perfect contracts that favor the writers in every way. But NOBODY in the industry wants to do business with these people or sign those contracts.

He also told me frankly: y'gotta make the guy on the other side of the desk think he's getting a great deal by working with you. There are lots of talented artists. The ones who get the deals are the ones who have wiggle room in their demands and hire attorneys to negotiate those deals on their behalf. Don't save $400 now by not being represented by counsel and sign a bad deal that will eventually cost you millions.

With your own publishing company, no contacts, no business skills, you'll continue running a nonprofit called "I have my own publishing company."

By giving away a little bit initially, and gaining some access and with it, success, you will be in a much better position to get a little more of the pie in your next negotiation. We don't think so in the heat of the moment, but there's always next time. And once you get some momentum going, people who ignored you will be parked on your lawn with limos and lobsters.

You build a career. Being a hit songwriter, band, or lyricist doesn't happen overnight. You'd like it to, I know, but take a breath and hoard chocolate. The realistic path to success goes like this: First, you take a songwriting class, learn your craft, write a hundred songs. After that, write a hundred more songs. At that point, you need a mentor like me to give you truthful, consistent feedback, and guide your career. You meet the folks, networking at every turn, and co-write with tunesmiths a little further up the ladder. You start getting some nibbles. Then you catch fire. It's a process.

I suggest to all my clients that they go to as many industry events as possible. The biannual ASCAP meetings and BMI meetings are great networking opportunities. Everybody they want to know and do business with is there.

The best event by far is the Grammys. I recommend you join the National Academy of Recording Arts and Sciences, thereby being eligible to buy tickets to that gala. Sure, it would be fun to just go and sit up in the rafters, but I urge you to save up and get really good seats, which would allow you to attend the inner circle after-party. Everybody who was nominated and everybody who won is present, along with their agents, managers, past life cuticle removers, and spiritual advisors/bookies.

I suggest that instead of saying, "Hi, my name is Molly Leikin and I'm a songwriter and I'd like to send you an mp3," I would use the evening to congratulate everybody, especially people who are not in the limelight, for the good job they've done. Nobody really knows the faces of music publishers other than the people in the music business. So if you walked up to the VP of Warner/Chappell and said, "I'm really proud of you. Congratulations on your success tonight. It's a great record. I always knew you had good ears. Good for you," they will remember you. Ask for a business card and trade for yours. Then, the very next day, send everyone you met the night before a handwritten personal note on nice stationery. Write something like, "Congratulations. I'm proud of you. It's a well-earned honor." Then a week later, call and say, "When your desk is clear, I'd love to talk to you about an exciting new project that we can do together."

Sounds cocky and arrogant, yes, but somebody might bite. See, everybody congratulates the stars just for tying their shoes, but in a music publishing company, the only thing anybody usually hears is what they've done wrong. So this would be a real change of pace and is something that would definitely attract the recipients' attention. They don't want to hear, "I've been sleeping with my eleven orphaned refugee children in a stolen car and my unemployment ran out at the same time my husband ran off with his brother-in-law's lyricist's hypnotist." I would confine my comments to, "I know we're going to make money and history together." The point is to make your approach from a position of power rather than need.

When music publishers turn us down, we think there are the enemy, but they're not. They need us and we need them. Without our new music, where would they be? Judy Harris, a music publisher in Nashville, told me this:

> "I encourage artists and writers alike to perform and write the best song they can write, remembering, at the same time, they don't have to have lived the song personally. It's just the best song they can find inside them at the moment."

My agent says, "You write because you love to write. You need to write. It's not about the money but if you do your job correctly you start getting hits." And ASCAP board members tell me this: "As for encouraging new artists, I would suggest two practical things in addition to continue working hard at your craft and improving your creative ability. Try to find your voice. Even as styles change around you, get to know your market and try to develop a very thick skin. The main thing is to do your art, no matter what. Nobody has the right to shut you down. You know you've got something special to contribute to the literature of music, and I can't wait to hear it."

Make a deal with yourself to be in it for the long haul. Otherwise, get a master's or doctorate in something for which there are acres of ads in ZipRecruiter or Indeed.com, and write because you love to write.

Your songs have extraordinary potential income streams. Get to work.

CHAPTER 11

GETTING YOUR SONGS PUBLISHED

As a consultant to lyricists, songwriters, and singer/songwriters, I receive a hundred emails a week from new tunesmiths all over the world, saying they want to get their songs published. They also ask how much it costs.

This is what I tell them: a legitimate music publisher will not charge you to publish your work. Only scuzz buckets do. Steer clear of the latter.

WHAT PUBLISHING A SONG REALLY MEANS

When my first song was published, I expected to see shiny sheet music with a nice picture on the cover, but I learned that when a song is published, unlike a book, what a songwriter gets is a signed contract, and maybe a small check. Heavy on the maybe. Sheet music isn't printed until later, when the song is a hit. At that point, a photo of the artist or band who recorded your song, making it a hit, will be on the cover. Your name will appear as well, but in small print.

No matter how small the font, you still get paid per copy sold. That amount varies from forty cents up. Everything is negotiable.

HOW DO I SELL MY SONGS?

Lots of new songwriters, singer/songwriters, and lyricists call me, saying they want to sell their songs. They don't know that's not how our industry works. Only sleezoids buy material, taking advantage of naïve writers who need instant gratification and recognition. And maybe ten bucks.

As in any business, there are scurrilous companies claiming to "buy" your work outright, but when you see one of their ads, as Tom Ganz and I wrote, "run away so fast you leave your shoes behind."

Suppose you do sell a song for ten dollars. What if that song goes on to earn $10,000,000? Your name will never appear on the credits, or copyright, and you'll never earn more than that initial ten dollars. EVER. No matter who you tell that it's your song, nobody will care or believe you. No attorney will take your case. It's over.

Don't sell your songs. Instead, you get them published and earn royalties.

You and your publisher are partners. They don't make any money from your songs until you do. You're a team. However, writers and publishers are often at odds. Publishers feel their writers demand instant placements and deals. Writers complain full-time when that doesn't happen and feel their publishers are not paying enough attention to them. It's like being a middle child.

This debate will never end. However, once you, as a songwriter, make your first deal through the efforts of your publisher, everybody loves everybody again. You share limos to the Grammys, name your children after one another, and then, when that positive wave subsides, go back to leaving dead possums on doorsteps.

HOW THE SONG ROYALTY PIE IS SHARED

Suppose a song is a circle, like a CD. Draw a line through the diameter. The top half is the songwriter's share. The bottom half is the publisher's share.

All new songwriters are desperate to find a publisher for their work. But there are publishers and there are publishers. You want a viable one, with recent hits and lots of current connections. A guy who placed a song on the B-side of a Snot single in the '70s is not your best shot now.

Even when you connect with a good publisher, in the real music business, you and that person will probably be at odds soon enough. But writers and publishers need each other. A publisher is only as good as their new talent. And although you, as a tunesmith, may think you're a hot shot and don't require a publisher's help, you do.

For the few years I published a handful of songs by very talented new artists, I got to see firsthand what a music publisher goes through. Although I placed 89 percent of these songs, when Miramax suspended production and froze all of their projects, there went my placements. My writers weren't interested in the whys.

I'd get calls on my private, unlisted line, in the middle of the night, demanding lists of other projects to which I'd pitched their tunes. I was bombarded by texts and emails saying it had been four days since we signed our agreement and where was their hit?

In the end, no matter how hard or long I'd pitched their material, or how many flights I took to meet with artists in Sugar Ditch, I simply returned the publishing rights to everybody's songs, and that was that.

It's tough out there, even with the hottest hustle and lifetime connections. So respect your publisher for trying to help you.

A SPECIAL THANKS

When somebody is especially nice to me, I send a handwritten note. It's rare for anyone in the music business to get a "nice job" pat on the back. So my gesture is noted. Try it. You'll be remembered as a good person, and that goes a long way in any business.

BILLBOARD

As a writer, it's part of your job to know who publishes the hit songs/artists in your genre each week. You can find all that information on the *Billboard* charts. Subscribe to that magazine online and make it part of your business responsibility to know who did what. There is no fairy godmother who will do that for you. The schlemiels who pretend to be this miracle really aren't. So it's on you until you've got enough momentum on your own, for a real manager, from a muscle company, who will bully their way into any deal for you. Before this happens, you have to prove to the manager that the time spent each day on you will be profitable in the short run.

So until you sign with a pushy, persistent manager, it's your responsibility. And if you don't do it, nothing will get done. Period. Don't hire someone to do it for you. You'll be sorely disappointed. Rev up your own hustle muscles.

While reading the chart in your genre, if you honestly feel you and your material are right for a particular publishing company working with a hit artist, contact someone there.

If the artist writes their own songs, don't bother submitting material to that company. They probably won't listen to outside material, let alone record it. Some artists are so lawsuit-prone, they're advised by their attorneys never to listen to any else's songs, especially someone they don't know.

The best way in is to co-write, and be "invited into the room" while an artist creates new material. That usually won't happen until you have some cred.

On the way there, be smart about submitting material. Before you go to the trouble of trying to penetrate an overloaded, cataclysmic publishing office, make sure all the acts they service aren't what we call "self-contained," recording songs they write for themselves.

Assuming a group in your genre doesn't write all of its own material, contact the publisher of their latest hit and find out who their professional manager is. That's the person who placed their most recent hit with them. Check the correct email address with the receptionist. If she doesn't trust you, tell her you need the information for some big shot (use a major player) for whom you're temping and need to update his/her address book. God will forgive you. Meanwhile, be very gracious to that receptionist. She's hassled all day, every day, and can use a friend.

Practice your phone pitch over and over in your mirror. Record it and listen back. When you're ready, your initial phone call will go something like this:

RECEPTIONIST

HOME OF THE HITS

YOU

Hi. Who am I speaking to?

RECEPTIONIST

Why?

YOU

I'm a hit songwriter. My name is Sonoma.
What's yours?

RECEPTIONIST

Please hold.

You're on hold. Stay there. She'll be back. Eventually.

RECEPTIONIST

HOME OF THE HITS. Hold on.

YOU

But...

Keep holding. Don't get mad. Stay calm. The little lady has all of her lines flashing at once. Imagine being her.

RECEPTIONIST

Home of the hits!

YOU

Hi, I'm Sonoma, and you are?

RECEPTIONIST

The receptionist.

YOU

Right. And a very good one. But what's your
name? You sound like a nice person.

RECEPTIONIST

> (softening a little)
> Maple. Please hold.

You've got eight seconds left before your phone battery dies, but you keep holding.

RECEPTIONIST

> Home of the hits!

YOU

> Hi, Maple. It's me, Sonoma. I'm a songwriter with a hit for Maren Morris. Nobody else in town has heard it yet. Since I see in *Billboard* that your company published Maren's last single, I'd like to meet with (the professional manager) and see if we can do business together and make some money.

RECEPTIONIST

> Can you hold?

You're dying to strangle the woman, but you keep your cool. In a week she could be running the label. Don't think that hasn't happened.

RECEPTIONIST

> Yeah?

YOU

> Maple, like I said, I've got a hit song right here for Maren Morris and...

RECEPTIONIST

> We don't listen to unsolicited material.

YOU

> This isn't just another unsolicited tune. I met (professional manager) at the ASCAP workshop a few weeks ago and she asked me to call as soon as I had something for one of her artists. I'm a professional songwriter. And I'm good. Please, Maple, I'd like your help and cooperation in putting me through to (professional manager).

RECEPTIONIST

> She's in a meeting.

YOU

> When can I call back?

RECEPTIONIST

> She's flying to New York in an hour. Two weeks there. Then Dar es Salaam. Plus the Yukon Territories.

YOU

> Thanks for her itinerary. I appreciate that,
> Maple. I'll give you a call a few days after she
> gets back.

RECEPTIONIST

> Then she's going to Sierra Leone and Guam.

You want to put your fist through a wall, but you bite your tongue, take a very deep breath, and cheerfully say you'll call back again. And you do.

Eventually you'll get through. As you listen to all the songs on the current top forty, realize those people finally got past the gatekeepers. So will you. Honest.

As you navigate the choppy waters of Musicland, make sure you're dealing with legitimate professionals all along the way and skip right over the grief. Save hard copies of all paperwork. I'd even suggest you put them in a safety deposit box. And never, ever trust anyone to do anything without a signed agreement. No matter what the deal is, get it in writing. If somebody you're dealing with won't do that, run the other way. Even a family member needs to sign paperwork. You can't imagine the drama when writers have hits and their fourth cousins who died five years ago want in.

You don't want to carry around a loser attitude for your whole career. Act like a winner, and you'll become one.

PUBLISHING SCAMS

Any time you file a copyright with the Library of Congress, there are companies monitoring each filing. These disreputables send each new copyright holder a form letter, saying you have outstanding, genius potential as a songwriter, and they want to do business with you. They may also include a publishing contract for the title you just registered.

Pretty thrilling when you live in East Chuch, and this is your first attempt at the business of music, right?

Wrong. It's a scam. Tear up the "contract."

To prove my point, from time to time, I send a lyric, with the full filing fee, for copyright, to the Library of Congress. This is what one of my recent lyrics said: "Whoa Whoa Whoa" for three double-spaced pages.

I got the same "genius" letter when filing the copyright for another of my original songs, called "Blank," which was a blank page.

So beware of being "discovered" by companies with access to all the information floating around the Library of Congress copyright office. The employees are exemplary. It's the scuzz buckets you need to avoid.

PUBLISHING GOLDEN EAGLE AWARDS

After pitching a song to an alleged song tip sheet, one of my clients, who was a radiologist, got a call in the middle of the night from a guy somewhere in the great unknown, saying my client had won a Golden Eagle Publishing Award for excellence in lyric writing. Really?

I called the company issuing the citation and asked what the prize was. "Prestige," I was told. "He can tell everybody he won a Golden Eagle, which will open a lot of doors."

Not so much.

I called a dozen people I'd been working with in the music business, and nobody ever heard of this company or its glamor prize. Further, in order to attend the dinner, my client had to pay $2,500 for his meal, but he got a free listing in the catalog. Whoopie.

As my grandmother would say, you need a Golden Eagle Award like you need another hole in your head.

AVOID CHEAP MUSIC-FOR-HIRE COMPANIES

There are plenty of other scams out there. Legions of smarmy companies prey on naïve, frustrated lyricists by offering to write and produce inexpensive "melodies" for those lyrics and even market the finished products. Not so fast.

On behalf of my clients, I've contacted most of these companies. What they offer sounds like a reasonable idea, but the reality is, the alleged original melodies are the same ones they sold thousands of times before, the singers are past their prime, sing flat and completely without feeling. None of the thousands of disappointed clients who have contacted me after the fact ever earned a penny. And all of these writers were offered the opportunity to be on a special compilation album, but only if they first coughed up thousands more dollars.

What?

You get what you pay for. If you pay $300 or $500 for a melody, that's what your tune sounds like. Lots and lots of other writers will get the same cheap and derivative tune for that same price. But if you work with a real composer, with contemporary chops, in the real world, with current recording equipment, then you have a shot. Nobody's looking for recycled songs, only original ones.

As a rule of thumb, if it sounds too good to be true, it probably is. I always urge my clients to check with me first before sending anything to anybody who charges publishing or inexpensive production fees in the music industry.

No matter what offer anybody makes, hire an entertainment lawyer in a major music city to review it for you, not a real estate attorney in The People's Republic of Nope. In spite of the convenience of email, pick up the phone. Invest in your career. Pay the lawyer. Nobody is interested in how broke you are or how many hip replacements your chidoodle needs. Speak to your lawyer directly. Send the contract for personal review. FAQs aren't going to do it for you.

Sometimes people posing as lawyers online, aren't. They say, "Our firm represents…" That's all well and good, but the firm could be engaged in a variety of nefarious activities that have nothing to do with copyright law and everything to do with "headin' upstate to do five to ten."

GET IT IN WRITING

I assume you've heard the expression, "anybody who represents himself has a fool for a client." It's rampant everywhere, especially in the music business. Here's the worst story I ever heard.

Here's a case of how hiring an attorney could have avoided a catastrophe.

A former songwriting client decided to have a baby rather late in her life. She bought some eggs from a UCLA student and sperm from a handsome artist. On her first try, she was pregnant. The baby was beautiful and healthy. Everybody loved her.

Much to our collective dismay, the first thing the songwriter did when announcing her baby's birth was apply for and get welfare benefits, since technically, the baby's father was "absent." That, apparently, is legal in California.

The baby was adorable, never stopped smiling, and everybody goo goo'd over her. I even wrote her theme song. However, my client and the egg donor never had an agreement in writing. They "trusted the Universe" to take care of everything. Right.

The egg donor and the songwriter happened to meet by accident at a Paul Simon concert. The baby was a clone of the egg donor, who decided she wanted the baby. Myriads of litigating later, the daughter was returned to the donor. Since there was no written agreement and the songwriter was on welfare, without any other means of supporting the child, the tunesmith lost.

This fracas didn't involve a song. It was much worse. From this example, you can see what happens when you don't memorialize your agreements in writing.

Songwriting is your life. Your songs are your children. Protect them. If you don't respect them, you have no business claiming to be an artist interested in successful commerce. The cheapest answer is just that. It's never the best. And certainly not the only one.

KEEP TRACK OF YOUR DEDUCTIONS

As soon as you start earning royalties, all expenses stemming from doing business in the music business, including production and attorney fees, are deductible from your taxes. Let's hope your royalties are so large, you'll need those deductions.

DEMAND YOUR FAIR SHARE

Lori Lieberman, an extremely talented artist and friend, who recorded "Killing Me Softly" as a teen, suggested the idea for that song to Charlie Fox and Norman Gimbel. She shared her notes, feelings, and experiences with Gimbel. But when the song appeared on her album, which Gimbel and Fox produced, her name was missing as co-writer.

When Lori insisted they do right by her and give her co-writing credit, they froze her out but wouldn't release her from their production contract. For four years, they prevented her from recording, publishing, or making production deals with anyone else. Gimbel and Fox had lots of money and power to fight Lori in court. She was new and just getting by. It wasn't fair. But that's how the little guy gets squashed.

In the end, even though the song was recorded thousands of times, generating millions of dollars a year in royalties, Lori was never credited as co-writer of "Killing Me Softly." However, the controversy never went away. And on the day Oscar-winning Norman Gimbel died, every obituary, in every news outlet on the planet, mentioned his dispute with Lori, instead of celebrating his extraordinary legacy.

Is that how you want to be remembered? Give credit where credit is due. Nobody's gonna care if you get 1 percent or 80 percent of a hit song. All they'll ever be concerned about is seeing your name on it.

My attorney, who negotiated my very first publishing deal, told me this: "I can't get you out of anything I didn't get you into." Neither, by the way, can anybody else.

THE PUBLISHER'S PUBLISHER

INTERVIEW WITH TIM WIPPERMAN

Although I always lived on the west coast and did business in Hollywood, I'd heard about Tim Wipperman and followed his career throughout my songwriting life. He was, is, and always will be, the go-to guy on Music Row.

When I was still a scuffler in Hollywood, publisher Artie Wayne sent one of my lyrics to Tim in Nashville. Tim handed the lyric to Larry Keith, one of his staff writers. Larry wrote the music to "Lucky Chicago," which was recorded by Jody Miller, and became my first county cut.

As many times as I went to Nashville to co-write, I never met Larry Keith. Or Tim. By then, I was signed to Chappell and that was that. But all these years later, Tim Wipperman appeared on my Facebook page. I'm grateful to him for hooking me up way back when, and for giving me this important interview for my book.

There wasn't a time in Tim Wipperman's life when he wasn't all about the music. In college, he played sax and worked his way through school playing R&B music in cover bands, performing hits by the likes of Otis Redding and Sam & Dave.

After visiting his cousin, songwriter Rory Bourke, in Nashville, although there was no call for Tim's instrument in Music City, he stayed. His roommate was Dave Conrad, the head of A&M Records in Nashville. At first, Tim volunteered for that company, learning the ropes of the music business. Then one day, Chet Atkins, also known as Mr. Guitar, walked right in, asking, "Do you guys know how to run a publishing company?"

In those days, Tim says, "We didn't know what we didn't know." So he replied, "Yes."

He worked his way through traditional, old school music publishing for Webb Pierce, whose guitar-shaped swimming pool still welcomes all tourists to Music Row. He did a stint at Cedarwood, working with writers like John D. Loudermilk and Mel Tillis. From there, he was hired by Bob Beckham at Combine, a great mentor. One writer signed there, who was just starting his career, was a tall, skinny guy with a Rhodes Scholarship named Kris Kristofferson.

It was a wonderful experience for Tim, working with Billy Swan, Johnny MacRae, Tony Joe White, and Shel Silverstein, who, in addition to writing songs, penned children's books, including *Where the Sidewalk Ends*.

From Combine, Tim went to Warner Brothers Music and stayed twenty-nine years. He'd probably still be there, except that the Bronfmans bought Warner Brothers and brought their own people in. So Tim began working with Clint Black and Little Big Town.

Then he struck gold again at Rezonant Music. According to Mediabase's year-end review, Rezonant Music Publishing had twenty-one of the top one hundred singles of the year. These songs included such hits as Ross Copperman's "Get Along"

(Kenny Chesney), Scooter Carusoe's "For the First Time" (Darius Rucker), Trevor Rosen's "Hotel Key" (Old Dominion), Hillary Lindsey's "Take Back Home Girl" (Chris Lane), and Mitch Rossell's "All Day Long" (Garth Brooks).

His writers didn't stop there. Matt Jenkins and Kevin Kadish wrote "Whiskey Glasses"; Hillary Lindsey, Lori McKenna, and Liz Rose wrote "Girl Crush"; and Tom Douglas, Scooter Carusoe, and Chris Janson wrote "Drunk Girl." Tim also represents the catalog of mega-writer Ross Copperman, who has written twenty-nine number one singles, including "Three Chords and the Truth."

"We Were Us," penned by Tim's writers Nicolle Galyon, Jimmy Rogers, Jimmy Robbins, and Jon Nite was a smash hit for Keith Urban and Miranda Lambert. Try NOT singing that one.

Unlike traditional music publishers, at Rezonant, Tim made deals with the majors. "We provided the funding to buy the catalogs and hire their staff. Our writers wanted to deal with their own creative teams. So did I.

"We had the cream of the crop. Song of the year, 'All About the Bass,' was by our Hillary Lindsey and Kevin Kadish, who wrote and produced it with and for Megan Trainor. (Megan was hired to sing the demo for Kevin. Twenty minutes later, she was signed as an artist.)"

As a publisher, Tim keeps asking himself what can be done that no one else has done before. When asked how he rises above the ambient noise, he says, "I never tell my writers what to write. I follow their lead. Under the Umbrella of Anthem, I am their president. My first priority is to build an environment conducive to our writers' success.

"We are associated with a remarkable group of songwriters who have created some of our most diverse and memorable songs. It is a testament to their creativity that artists who are at the top of their respective games turn to us when looking for a great song to cut and take to their fans.

"While some may think it will be a challenge to top such a great year, I've heard some of the new songs that these incredibly talented writers are working on and have no doubt they will see even greater success this time next year."

Rezonant Music Publishing became Anthem Music Publishing. And collectively, Tim's staff writers have won "north of five hundred ASCAP and BMI Country Music Awards."

There's a music publisher who knows how to nurture and make the right business connections for his writers. He came up through the ranks, did a great, creative job along the way, knows everybody, and is respected up and down Music Row. We can all learn from his journey.

Thank you, Tim, for being you.

CHAPTER 12

MAKING MONEY IN THE MEANTIME

I hold a BA in French literature, along with a master's in fine art. I am personable, clean up nice, and after college, probably could have gotten any job I wanted. But I was a songwriter. I had no interest in developing something called software, to track down missing, striped, left foot, green socks in the Outer Hebrides.

My French language skills were excellent, so people were pushing me to become a translator at the UN. But hey, I was afraid of getting one word wrong and boom goes London.

So I typed for a living, writing and getting A+s for my friends' master's theses in architecture, sneezing, and the psychology of bark. I charged six dollars an hour, and whenever I felt like it, I could write a song.

Like me back then, you need a day job. I know you hate to hear this, but you do. Life is expensive. So is making music. Cars break down. Rent goes up, like car insurance and Dodger's tickets. You need a day job, but only until your music jackpot clangs.

Although the struggling artist has been romanticized in movies and books, it's no fun being poor. I was. For a long time.

And I don't recommend it. But while you're going after it and are aching for your first big yes, here are some suggestions to keep your bills current.

INTERNSHIPS

All entertainment companies, publishers, recording studios, movie and TV studios, and post- production houses need interns. Talented people fight to the death to be considered to work eighteen-hour days for no pay. It's a little easier to land one of these gigs if you're John Legend's nephew twice removed. But if you're not, you still have a shot.

There's a legend about David Geffen applying for a position in the mail room at the William Morris Agency, claiming he was a UCLA grad. A degree in something was essential to be considered for the job. Truthfully, he'd parked his car on campus once to attend a Whomp concert, but a degree? Not so much. Nonetheless, those executives at William Morris were expecting proof of David's degree. So he had to chase down the letter from UCLA saying his bachelor of communications degree was bogus.

I'm not suggesting you do that. You lie, you die. But you can't take a number and politely wait your turn. A little moxie couldn't hurt. When you do get a job as an intern, it's your chance to show the powers that be how reliable you are. You're smart. You're the first one in, the last one out. You're nice to everyone and make an important contribution, even if, at first, it's locating the prime source for stolen vanilla beans from Northern Madagascar for the executives' café au double latte with just a soupcon of cinnamon. With your dedicated work ethic, when the next paying job opens up, it'll probably be yours.

Once you're "inside," you will make connections that will make connections that will hook you up for your whole life. And at some point, the music people you've been aching to meet will return your calls.

CASUALS AND CUSTOM SONGWRITING

Since you already write songs, and probably do casuals on weekends, why not add custom songwriting to your resume? Write tunes especially for the bride and groom or Bat Mitzvah girl. A few hundred extra dollars a few times a week makes a big difference during your scuffling days.

COPYWRITING

If you're good with words, I recommend becoming a copywriter at an ad agency. That's a place where clever is celebrated. It sure beats typing. And many agencies have a music department. Some of the bigger ones include jingles in the services they offer their clients. Offer to help, but don't take over. Whatever you do, don't push somebody out of his/her job.

Even if, at first, you're only doing cannabis runs for the junior choir director at Our Lady of the Angels Cathedral, at least you're there. Someone will quit. Having been on site for a few months, you could get her/his job. People love to work with people they know. They're always suspicious of strangers.

TEACH

Suppose you're a virtuoso guitarist or keyboard genius. You could teach. I know that's not what you practice twelve hours a day to do, but it's a gig. Giving private lessons is lucrative. And one happy little Fender-playing, tone deaf, toothless kid from Beverly Hills can get you a lot of business. Hey—you could become the go-to guy for flamenco or dirty rock 'n' roll. And, the parents of "gifted" children could have interesting careers, some of which might be in the entertainment business.

Meanwhile, while you're exploring alternative sources of income within the writing and music fields, you're sharpening your writing skills. You're learning to tailor your songs to specific requirements, which is what you will have to do when writing for a particular artist.

Who knows when you'll bump into someone during your hungry days who wants a real song? If you're used to writing on assignment, you'll be ready for anything and will do a good job. Satisfied customers will come back to you for more. What you're doing here is taking charge of your life, creating cash flow, and gaining confidence as a writer. That last item, confidence, is the most important attribute you have for sale, both to yourself and to prospective customers.

HOLD MUSIC

I've banked with the same institution all my life. My bank used to be small, then was absorbed by an impersonal corporation, and is still using the same four-bar hold "music." I have to fortify myself with party-size bags of chocolate before ever attempting to call in. And I've flown all over the country to talk to various executives about making their hold music more fun. I even offered to produce it with some of the best musicians in the world. However, as of this morning, not a quarter note has changed.

I think I've pretty well put in my time trying to change this. So it's on one of you now to step up and go after it. Not only will you save humanity from screaming and grinding your teeth down to your shoulders, but there's some major money to be made. You could even feature new singer/songwriters.

Keep me in the loop.

WRITING JINGLES THAT SELL

INTERVIEW WITH JIM ANDRON

For a minute, Jim Andron and I were in the trenches together in Hollywood. We tried writing a few songs together that didn't take, and all these years later, we hooked up on Facebook.

I was happy to hear Jim had a great career writing jingles. Not just one here and there every five years or so, but he actually had a contract, a deal, and a salary.

When he tapped his songwriting well dry, he worked for Disney, producing albums for Disney Records. His project was *Rainbow Brite*, a kids' TV show. They were based on story books for kids to listen to in the car. Jim arranged and produced that music.

Then Disney decided they liked Jim's arranging more than his songwriting, so he did some symphonic background cues, which was basically library music. They gave him a budget, and whatever he could do under budget, he could keep. At that time, there was no Pro Tools. He hired live, talented musicians. Although he never received royalties (that's another story), his ASCAP statements were fat for many years. He wasn't any good at networking or glad-handing, but he was fortunate to hook up with people who were.

For example, there was a car dealership in Oregon. His marketing partner found the gigs. Then Jim did the jingles for their competitors. And he recorded everything in LA, working quickly and producing a quality product.

Jim told me there were car dealerships all over the country for which he did a lot of plug-ins, inserting names like Lake Las Vegas, James Madison University, athletic departments, political jingles, station IDs, top forty packages, country packages, R&B packages—but mostly client jingles.

"The company I worked for had six salespeople who'd go out into those small towns across America and sign clients for a year with the local radio station. In exchange, the clients got free jingle packages."

Later, when he and his partner sold the business, they had airtime that they'd turn around and sell to national advertisers like Gold Bond and Pepsi.

Jim told me, "I did the production. Andy Mark was the business guy. When I flew to Philly to meet him, the minute we shook hands we hit it off. So my family and I moved to Philadelphia. It was a Godsend—good schools, safe community in the burbs, my kids could play unsupervised outdoors. And Andy was a straight shooter. He said he'd pay me, and he did."

Then his company was bought by Premiere Radio Networks. Soon, Premiere was bought by Jacor. Jacor was purchased by Clear Channel, which is now iHeartRadio.

"I made a good salary," Jim told me. "My job was to write jingles. I wrote one a day for a year. This was before the internet. But I embraced every bit of technology as it came along. In the beginning, it used to take ten days to get approval. Then it switched to ten minutes.

"When I moved to Philly, my equipment took up half an eighteen-wheeler. Thirty years later, when I moved from Philly to Palm Desert, everything fit in two boxes.

"Our customers were half-price lawyers in Las Vegas, funeral parlors, dot-coms, local furniture stores, jewelry shops, real estate salesmen, shopping malls, Whole Foods. I could write a jingle for anybody."

I asked Jim what it takes to be a good jingle writer.

"First, you need to write hooks—fast, no-fluff hooks. Bam. Two lines in, six lines in the middle, two lines out. The middle notes are often removed for copy, but the two lines in and out stay. Commercials are traditionally twenty seconds, thirty seconds, sixty seconds. It's a very disciplined art form."

Jim supported himself and his family very comfortably for thirty years. Then his business partner died. The company was sold and Jim wasn't needed any longer. But he had a great thirty years.

Somebody's gotta pick up where he left off. Why not you?

CHAPTER 13

BOUNCING BACK

It's important for all lyricists, songwriters, singer/songwriters, and bands to remember that even the most successful of their heroes and colleagues have suffered enormous defeats, setbacks, and failures.

But they bounced back.

I've had publishers throw me out of their offices, yelling, "Gimme something I can dance to." And just a few months later, those same songs received standing ovations at Carnegie Hall. So who's right? The publisher knew what he could place, and the artist performing at Carnegie Hall sang what showed off her voice. So you need to know what people are looking for and pitch accordingly.

All artists suffer from rejection. Each of us feels stabbed at the time and inevitably retreats to a safe place under the bed, with massive amounts of chocolate, until we work through the pain, can remember who we are, and that there is artistic and commercial value in what we've created. Our work might just be positioned in the wrong segment of the marketplace for the moment.

All my favorite painters, authors, dancers, sculptors, tunesmiths, and composers have suffered highs and lows in their careers. It's gratifying to know they made it through and created their best work at the end of that long, bleak tunnel of nothin'.

I have a million rejection stories of my own. The best one, with the happiest ending so far, has to do with my song called "I Hear Your Heart."

Here's what happened. I was collaborating with a new singer/songwriter in Santa Barbara. Usually, I only worked with tunesmiths who were advanced in their careers, but what the heck. She had a strong singing voice. We had written two sensational songs together. I wrote lyric three and gave it to her, thinking she'd love it. Instead, I got a nasty email saying, "That's the worst thing I've ever seen. I couldn't possibly sing this. It's demeaning. I'll go blind if I have to see those words again. BTW: I can't possibly work with you again. I'm outta here."

Oh? I guess that was a no.

As disappointed as I was, I knew my lyric was especially good and figured someday I'd find a project needing it, although I had no idea how far out that someday might be. So I put my lyric aside, growled for a couple of days, and went on with the rest of my life.

Two years later, I was invited to participate in a collaboration with some European tunesmiths who wanted English lyrics for tracks recorded by a Latvian star named Raimonds Pauls. *Who?* I checked him out. He was a very big deal in the Balkans. The what? Not exactly Keith Urban, but hey, y'never know.

We made an agreement for the Europeans to create eight tracks, to which I'd write English lyrics. Seemed straightforward enough.

We completed seven very good songs but came up empty on number eight. My European colleagues kept sending tracks that I didn't feel would work in the USA. So, I finally suggested I write the eighth lyric first, to which they could write a melody, and I'd help with the stresses, since English wasn't their first language.

Out of the drawer comes "I Hear Your Heart," which they hated. Oy. So I sent them five more lyrics, none of which made them happy either. My work seemed to be doing more damage to international relations than Putin. At one point, I expected the FBI at my door to arrest me for subversive musical activities. Meanwhile, I had made a commitment I wanted to keep, took a lot of yoga classes, and climbed most of the trails in the Santa Ynez mountains, hoping for a solution that would make everybody happy.

Cut to a homeless kid sleeping on the couch of my European co-writer's office in Riga, Latvia. Not exactly Music City. Couch boy refused to leave until the composer listened to his CD. I'll always be grateful to this determined young man, who fished my discarded lyric out of the trash while he was waiting for the composer to listen to his work. A few weeks later, my assistant was going through the email and found an mp3 with that kid singing my lyric a cappella, and the song was fantastic.

Apparently, the young man was in a group called Cosmos, and they had some kind of a label deal in the Balkans, and the next thing I knew, I was getting phone calls in the middle of the night from people with thick, Slavic accents, trying to tell me our song was a finalist in Eurovision.

A finalist in what?

I didn't know what that contest was, but I gleefully and triumphantly discovered that it's like American Idol. However, instead of representing just one country, Eurovision is for forty-two.

According to my ASCAP checks, being a finalist is a very big deal. All those previous noes, including the one from that still-unsigned writer in Santa Barbara, turned into a big yes, and I had another season in the sun.

All of my colleagues—all of *your* colleagues—have stories like these. The bottom line is persistence. If you stick with it and continue to write strong, chart-appropriate, original songs, your time will come.

A writer's job is to write. If you do that, keep raising the level of your craft and write your fingerprint, and hustle your hustle, someday, the world will know your work. But until then, I want you to feel in your bones that you have the magic to go the distance. No Grammy can give that to you. Honestly, you have to give it to yourself, every day, all day, for the rest of your life.

People get hot and cold. When you heat up, it's because you created the heat, hung out with the right people, and stayed in the game. When you're cold, don't fall into the trap of thinking somebody took something away from you. I have colleagues who've gone from Teslas to skateboards and back. Some are hitchhiking in Gucci shoes and will drive home next year in Bentleys stuffed with *Billboard* Music Awards.

As artists, we don't live in straight lines. We don't get lucky and stay lucky forever. It's a roller coaster called the Music Business. If you want to ride along with us, take your ticket and be prepared.

Write well. Surprise me. Dazzle me. I'm counting on it. You are the future of music. The world needs your songs.

Please don't let us down.

Love,

Molly

STUFF AT THE BACK OF THE BOOK

I. How to schedule a personal, private Zoom or whatever's next phone call with Molly Leikin.

If you connected with me while reading this book, I invite you to schedule a one-on-one telephone, Zoom, or whatever's next Song Consultation with me to review your work in terms of the current marketplace. If it's a good fit, I will hook you up with everyone I know looking for your fingerprint. That's included in my fee.

If your material isn't quite ready, I'll give you personal, professional, and very specific feedback on how to tweak what you do so it can realistically compete with the very best lyrics, songs, bands, and singer/songwriters out there. Something like: move that up here, say this twice, try this line down here, try a C instead of G so the range isn't so tough....

That's all included in my Consultation fee, which is based on the number of lyrics/songs/tracks you want to send me. Just go to songmd.com

Please note: I work by Consultation only. For legal reasons, any material arriving in my office that is not from a client who pays my consulting fee, must, regrettably, be deleted immediately. Thank you for respecting the professional parameters of this consultancy.

That said, please set up your consultation through my website, www.songmd.com.

2. Molly-Ann Leikin's Master Class in Songwriting, MP3-CD edition.

Approximately 6.5 hours

This is a collection of the best Master Classes in Songwriting I taught at UCLA. It is a complete home-study hit songwriting course—step by step from basic song structure, lyric writing, co-writing, muscle marketing, to promoting your hit songs everywhere!

Order your copy here: songmd.com/mollystore

OTHER CREATIVE STUFF

Using our imaginations, we can create many magical things, not only songs. Between now and the next edition of this book, I'd like someone to please invent the following:

1. Snap-in replacement vertebra

2. Drag-and-drop software to move rain clouds from flooded areas to all the places on Earth experiencing drought. While you're at it, design this program so a smart meteorologist can insert some kind of a whatchamacallit into the eye of hurricanes to diffuse them.

3. An instant way to un-miss the bad guys.

4. Microwave ovens that will stop beeping when you tell them you'll be there in a sec.

5. Love that doesn't hurt.

If It Rains On You

(Charlie Black/Molly-Ann Leikin)

It's a good day for travelling
But not for goodbye
You and I sure do have
Stories to tell
Got an old silver dollar
Says I'll see you again
Until then, I know
You're gonna do well.
Keep your back to the wind
Keep your face to the sun
Keep a dream in your pocket
Just in case you need one
You can take my love with you
Like a dime in your shoe
Then you'll know who to call on
If it rains on you.

© Warner/Chappell Music

Write well today and do yourself proud.

ABOUT THE AUTHOR

Credit: David Gersch

Molly Leikin was born in Canada and defected with her baritone ukulele to California during a fifty-eight-below-zero blizzard. The Department of Public Social Services in Los Angeles seemed to think she'd be a good Emergency Intake worker.

Yeah, right.

But it was a day job. And all of Molly's clients claimed the father of their babies was a rockstar, so it was Molly's responsibility to go after the alleged deadbeat dads for child support. However, instead of Molly helping the underprivileged get off welfare, they got *her* into the music business.

Starting as a staffwriter at Almo Music (A&M Records), over the next ten years, Molly had her songs recorded by almost every pop and country artist on the *Billboard* charts. Now she has a house full of gold and platinum records, plus an Emmy nomination. She has written with and for everybody from Katy Perry to Cher, Tina Turner, Anne Murray, Placido Domingo, Glen Campbell, Billy Preston—even Yitzi Ya Ya and the Yo Yo's. Molly has also written themes and songs for more than six dozen TV shows and movies, including *Violet*, which won an Oscar.

The author of *How to Write a Hit Song* (six editions), *How to Be Hit Songwriter*, and *How to Make Good Song A Hit Song* (did you notice the theme here?), using her boundless ingenuity, Molly also created Songwriting Consultants, Ltd., the international song consulting firm, where she's mentored two generations of Grammy winners and nominees. She also launched Anything with Words, her custom speechwriting company, whose clients include CEOs, CFOs, and UFOs.

Molly practices yoga, takes long walks as the sun comes up, collects contemporary art, flosses, and lives in Santa Barbara.

You can reach Molly here: songmd@songmd.com